LEARNING AND
A LIBERAL EDUCATION

PETER R. H. SLEE

Learning and a liberal education

THE STUDY OF MODERN HISTORY IN THE UNIVERSITIES OF OXFORD, CAMBRIDGE AND MANCHESTER, 1800–1914

 Manchester University Press

Published by MANCHESTER UNIVERSITY PRESS
Oxford Road, Manchester M13 9PL
and 27 South Main Street, Wolfeboro, N.H. 03894-2069, U.S.A.

British Library cataloguing in publication data
Slee, Peter R. H.
   Learning and a liberal education: the study of modern history in the
   Universities of Oxford, Cambridge and Manchester, 1800–1914.
   1. History – Study and teaching (Higher) – England – History – 19th
   century
   I. Title
   907'.1142   D16.4.G7

Library of Congress cataloging in publication data
Slee, Peter R. H.
   Learning and a liberal education.

   Bibliography: p. 165.
   Includes index.
   1. Education, Higher – England – History – 19th
century. 2. University of Oxford – History – 19th
century. 3. University of Cambridge – History – 19th
century. 4. University of Manchester – History – 19th
century. I. Title.
LA636.7.S55   1986   378.42   86–18253

ISBN 0–7190–1896–X hardback

Photoset in Linotron Joanna by
Northern Phototypesetting Co., Bolton
Printed in Great Britain
by Bell and Bain Ltd., Glasgow

CONTENTS

PREFACE

The following pages are intended as a contribution to the history of higher education. Their creative impulse lies deep in a sense of curiosity aroused initially by the writer's own undergraduate studies. Table talk in the junior common room often took, and perhaps takes still, the speculative form of a guessing game. What *was* the purpose of a university education in the modern age? Further, could any such direction be found in or ascribed to the composition of a syllabus for which teachers taught and students read, often assiduously, but more often without any apparent sense of conviction about its educational value? This book makes no claim to provide direct answers to the problems pressing those who direct our own system of higher education, in which each, it seems, must seek his own salvation, but looks rather at the questions of value and purpose with which teachers and students were confronted in the years between 1800 and 1914.

ACKNOWLEDGEMENTS

The sources for this subject are abundant, but my own highly selective path through them has been made easier by the specialist knowledge and advice of Miss Ruth Vyse, Deputy Keeper of the Archives at the Bodleian Library; Dr Peter McNiven, University Archivist at the John Rylands University Library of Manchester; the late Dr Peter Hunter-Blair, formerly Librarian of Emmanuel College, Cambridge; Mr Michael Halls, Archivist at King's College, Cambridge; Mr Underwood, Archivist at St John's College, Cambridge; Mr Kaye, lately Assistant Librarian at Trinity College, Cambridge; Mr Quinn of Balliol College, Oxford; Mrs L Topliffe of Exeter College, Oxford; Mr Burgass of Merton College, Oxford; and Mrs Dalton of New College, Oxford.

Though many of the materials used in this study are available on the open shelves of most good academic libraries, it seemed that for the purpose of my own research a good deal more was wheeled, fetched and carried by an army of ever-patient, ever-helpful, ever-courteous library staff. For their help in this respect I should like to thank Mr Waller of the Manuscript Room, and the staff of the Rare Books Room in the University Library, Cambridge; Mrs Searby at Emmanuel College Library, and the staff of the Duke Humfrey Room at the Bodleian Library, Oxford.

For kind permission to use and to quote from the sources listed in the bibliography I should like to thank the Master and Fellows of Emmanuel College, Cambridge; the Provost and Fellows of King's College, Cambridge; the Master and Fellows of Trinity College, Cambridge; the Rector and Fellows of Exeter College, Oxford; the Warden and Fellows of New College, Oxford; the Keepers of the Archives at the Universities of Oxford and Cambridge; Mr Herbert Tout; the Director of the Institute of Historical Research, and the President and Fellows of the Royal Historical Society.

I have benefited greatly from discussions with many friends and colleagues, particularly Dr Michael Brock, Dr John Breuilly, Mr Mark Curthoys, Mr N. B. Harte, Dr Ian Kershaw, Professor T. O. Ranger, Dr Mike Rose, Mr G. H. Slee, Dr Julia Smith, Professor Richard Southern and Dr Gillian Sutherland. I owe much more than I can record to the advice and direction of Professor Owen Chadwick and Dr Richard Tuck, who both assumed the mantle of supervisor during my studies in Cambridge. Needless to say, the shortcomings and failings of this work are entirely my own.

This work was undertaken with the financial assistance of a DES studentship, a British Academy Thank-offering to Britain Research Fellowship and an ESRC post-doctoral research fellowship. To these bodies I express my gratitude. As a research student at Emmanuel College, Cambridge, a tutor at Hulme Hall, Manchester, an associate member of Nuffield College, Oxford, and an ESRC post-doctoral research fellow in the Department of History at the University of Manchester I could not have wished to work in more congenial surroundings. I am grateful to my many friends in these institutions for their fellowship.

But my greatest debt is to my wife and to my parents. Without their love, patience and encouragement I could never have completed this work, and it is to them that I offer it in dedication.

INTRODUCTION

Four years' residence at an Oxford college has always been a costly business. Never more so than in the 1850s, when the sober young man of thrifty habit and sound schooling would run up bills of over £150 a year.[1] Few fathers could afford to regard a university education lightly. Fewer still did so. When considering the returns likely to accrue from such a considerable investment in their son's future the question would be raised, what is the point of a university education? Mr Verdant Green senior asked it and found there was no simple answer. The university was self-professedly a multi-functional body and 'a university career might' therefore 'be looked at from more than one point of view'.[2] It might be a finishing school of manner and taste, forming the character, moulding beliefs. It might train the mind, developing its capacity for analysis and argument. It might be the route to preferment, or perhaps the established path to the bar, the Church, or medical practice. It might in some cases prove an introduction to scholarship or science. Those who could pay could make of it what they would. Within certain well defined limits the university was a safe, controlled environment for the freeplay of the individual disposition.

But some found the limits chafing. The ancient universities were not without their critics. Some claimed they should reflect and contribute to rapid developments in science and scholarship; others that they should seek actively to develop in undergraduates the skills necessary to the continuing efficiency of British industry.[3] The universities, however, were autonomous. They directed their own affairs. And while there were always a good many ideas about what the universities *ought* to be doing only those held in consensus by their governing bodies were effective in influencing what they actually *did*.

This general consensus within a university of its overall purpose – what Edward Shils calls the 'academic ethos'[4] – acted as a mechanism for filtering and evaluating ideas about what was or was not an appropriate form of educational activity. It defined the broad limits within which the practical business of education could feasibly be conducted, and it therefore exercised direct bearing on the range of educational provision made formally accessible to students. Any meaningful discussion about extending the type, level or quality of provision was either conducted within the matrix of the academic ethos, or else began by proposing a modification of it.

How, then, in the early years of the nineteenth century did the universities of Oxford and Cambridge arrive at a coherent assessment of their function and purpose? In what relation did the academic ethos stand with academic practice? To what extent, in what ways and for what reasons did the two universities modify or redefine their assessment of their proper relationship with the intellectual and social world? How were these changing attitudes expressed in the practical business of teaching and study? These questions directed the research upon which this book is based.

The dynamics of academic practice are complex. But it is important that their complexity be recognised and demonstrated. Too often studies in the history of education have fallen victim to a crude form of functionalism which specifies that society gets what society wants from education when society wants it; or that the tracts of educational theorists influence in some direct (yet unspecified) way the form of educational practice. Too often the couplets 'education and society', 'theory and practice', are little more than labels that presuppose a relationship rarely made explicit.[5]

By what method, then, are the interrelationships between ideas about the nature, scope and purpose of higher education and the mechanisms in differing universities of considering, implementing and conducting new forms of educational practice to be uncovered and explained? One important consideration has influenced the approach adopted in this book. It is that good comparative histories of the English universities are rare indeed. This is not because comparisons are invalid or impossible to make, but rather because they are difficult to establish and sustain. There are two reasons for this.

First, universities are complex, highly individual institutions with their own distinctive character. Despite the generic name held in common, differences abound and are often more pronounced than similarities. This is as true of Oxford and Cambridge – which cannot seriously be regarded as regional branches of the same exclusive club – as it is of the civic universities. The Victoria University collapsed because its constituent colleges could no longer agree on the best methods of developing the practical business of higher education in all its forms. University College Liverpool, Owens College Manchester and the Yorkshire College at Leeds were different products of local pride, local spirit and local endeavour.[6]

Second, the bulk and range of material available for consultation are enormous. Still largely untapped and unsorted, it means that the thorough research upon which sound statements can meaningfully be based is an exciting, often pioneering yet ungovernably time-consuming process. How sad, then, that so often, in the mad, undignified scramble to publish, thorough research is bypassed, virgin archives are overlooked and ignored. Sad, because ultimately it is the discipline that suffers. The study of the history of education is blighted by a proliferation of 'histories' resting precariously on reminiscence and anecdote, loose generalisation and crude, functionalist assumptions. In the words of Professor Stubbs, 'what wonder that there are few who love it for its own sake, when there are so few who know it as it is.'[7]

The best comparative histories display the same basic approach. They limit their scope and concentrate on one aspect of educational provision, change or growth common to all the institutions involved, and study it in depth. Research is undertaken in sufficient detail to enable the author to make sound comparative judgements, while in breadth enough to avoid the charge of parochialism and lessen the risk of erroneous hypothetical abstraction.[8]

This book adopts the case study method. It analyses the dynamics of academic practice through an in-depth study of the emergence and growth of history as an Honours subject in the ancient, traditional universities of Oxford and Cambridge, and the youthful civic university of Manchester in the years between 1848 and the outbreak of war in 1914. These three institutions were the first in England to develop history as a rigorous and independent academic subject, and they responded to the challenge in strikingly different ways. Until the Great War and the emergence in London of a well organised and highly distinctive school of history, they remained unmatched for the size and the quality of their graduate output.

Their very different approaches to the systematic organisation and teaching of history were adopted as guiding posts for the newer schools, which, said Charles Firth in 1913, 'are as yet too recent to have produced much effect on the development of historical studies'.[9]

Why history? History was among the most vital intellectual and cultural forces in nineteenth-century England. The Victorians took history seriously. It was considered relevant; by some the key component in a new political technology, by others as a social and cultural cohesive. Its suggested relevance underlay its introduction into the university curriculum in 1848 but, under the prevailing academic ethos, also ensured that it occupied a lowly position among the studies of the university.[10]

But history was also a major intellectual growth industry. Standards of scholarship were constantly being improved, new areas of study opened up, new interpretations being made. The emergence of history as a research-oriented and therefore developing discipline was a source of constant pressure on the custodians of both curriculum and syllabus. In tandem with the developments in the philological and physical sciences it undermined the view that the well defined objectives of higher education could be met only through the dissemination of an unchanging corpus of cultural knowledge. But refined technical advances led later in the century to clashes between notions of 'service' to society and the academic duty to display the highest notions of contemporary scholarship in the syllabus. Different solutions to this common problem were reached by different institutions and for ostensibly different reasons.

Further, the changing interpretation of history as a means of education is an interesting process. But it lacks its historian. There are numerous reasons for this, not least the charge that the subject is hardly capable of historical treatment. It is claimed, and not without substance, that the enterprise is inherently 'whiggish', that it can be conducted only through an inverted teleological telescope which distorts as much as it discovers. It is said that the historian must be drawn inevitably to seek the origins of some present theoretical consensus of the discipline, to applaud precursors as heroes, to denounce obstructionist villains and to ignore non-contributors.[11] These dangers are very real. But they are attendant on the study of any contemporary institution with its roots in a past age, and they pervade studies of politics, social change and women's rights as much as they do studies of schools, colleges and universities. But such dangers can and usually are avoided by the historian who is aware of them and refuses to treat the past as an undeveloped image of the present.

It may be that the past is another country with whose language we will never completely be familiar, but if this book stimulates discussion and scholarship which improves on its own vocabulary I shall not be disappointed.

NOTES TO INTRODUCTION

1 James Heywood, The Recommendations of the Oxford University Commissioners (London, 1853), p. 204.

2 Cuthbert Bede, (pseud.), The Adventures of Mr. Verdant Green (1853, new ed. Oxford, 1982), p. 12.

3 See particularly the Edinburgh Review, pp. 9–10 following.

4 Edward Shils, Tradition (London, 1981), p. 182.

5 For a splendid discussion of these problems see Gillian Sutherland, 'The study of the history of education', History, LIV (1969), 49–59. For examples of the problem see Sheldon Rothblatt, Tradition and Change in English Liberal Education: an Essay in History and Culture (London, 1976), passim, but especially p. 196, and R. G. McPherson, Theory of Higher Education in Nineteenth Century England (Athens, N.Y., 1959), passim.

6 For examples of generic lumping see T. W. Heyck, The Transformation of Intellectual Life in Victorian England (London, 1982), ch. 3, ch. 6; Sheldon Rothblatt, The Revolution of the Dons: Cambridge and Society in Victorian England (London, 1968) (second ed. London, 1981), p. 2.

7 W. Stubbs, 'Inaugural (7 Feb 1867)', in Seventeen Lectures on the Study of Medieval and Modern History (Oxford, 1887), pp. 1–28 (28).

8 R. O. Berdahl, British Universities and the State (London, 1959); Michael Sanderson, The Universities and British Industry, 1850–1970 (London, 1972), but, best of all, R. A. Anderson, Education and Opportunity in Victorian Scotland (Oxford, 1983).

9 Though University College, Liverpool, and the Yorkshire College, Leeds, prepared candidates for the Victoria University BA degree in history their graduate output was dwarfed by that of Owens College, the other constituent part of the university. Between 1882 and 1904, when the university was dissolved, Owens produced fifty-four graduates in History to Liverpool's nine and Leeds's four. Administration of the joint school was dominated by Owens, first by Ward and then by Tout. Only forty-nine students from Leeds University (an average of about five a year) and thirty-two from Liverpool (an average of about three) graduated with BAs in history before 1914. History was taught at London University from the 1830s but only as an incidental part of the English module for the BA degree. It did not become a module in its own right until 1896 and developed into a separate school in 1904. It attracted few students – see A. F. Pollard, 'The University of London and the study of history', in Factors in Modern History (third ed., 1932), pp. 234–320 – and did not really take off until after the Great War; see N. B. Harte, One Hundred and Fifty Years of History Teaching at University College London (London, 1982), p. 25. Sheffield began teaching history on the Oxbridge model in 1908. Only eight students graduated before 1914, one more than Bristol, which began to offer degrees in history in 1910. Durham did not teach history as a separate subject

leading to a degree until after the war, while Birmingham, which did, had no takers.
No students graduated in history from there before the war.
    10   See pp. 9–18 following.
    11   Stefan Collini, Donald Winch and John Burrow, *That Noble Science of Politics: a Study*
    There are some articles chronicling the administrative changes in the regulations
for history degrees at individual institutions; J. O. McClachlan, 'The origins and early
development of the Cambridge Historical Tripos', *Cambridge Historical Journal*, 9
(1947–49), 78–105; G. Kitson Clark, 'A hundred years of the teaching of history at the
University of Cambridge, 1873–1973', *Historical Journal*, 16 (1973), 535–53; C. H. Firth,
Modern History in Oxford, 1841–1918 (London, 1920). The best piece on history as an
academic discipline is R. W. Southern, 'The shape and substance of academic history',
in *The Varieties of History from Voltaire to the present*, ed. Fritz Stern (London, 1970), 403–23,
which, delivered as an inaugural lecture at the University of Oxford, concentrates on
that university.

PART ONE

'Order,
unity and guidance'
THE EXPANDING
CURRICULUM, 1800–67

CHAPTER 1

'An elevated tone and a flexible habit of mind'
THE IDEA OF A LIBERAL EDUCATION, 1800–50

The universities are never without their critics. The ideals of a university education and the nature of a university's studies are brought continually into question by the society it purports to serve, never more dramatically perhaps than at the end of the eighteenth century.

The extent to which teaching and learning fell into abeyance in Georgian times has not yet been adequately or accurately determined. the standard interpretation – that of Gillray, Gibbon and Vicesimus Knox, portraying torpor, indolence, vice and a general dearth of learning has been challenged. Knox and his fellow critics based their invective on the formal requirements the university demanded of the student before he was awarded his degree. These, it was said, were performed 'in so negligent a manner, that it is equally impossible they should contribute to the advancement of learning, to the improvement or reputation of the candidate, or to the honour of the university'.[1] The examination system was undoubtedly open to abuse. We are told that:

> Mr John Scott took his Bachelors Degree in Hilary Term on the 20th February 1770. 'An examination for a Degree of Oxford', he used to say, 'was a farce in my time. I was examined in Hebrew and in History: 'What is the Hebrew for the place of a skull?' I replied, 'Golgotha.' 'Who founded University College?' I stated, (though, by the way, the point is sometimes doubted) that 'King Alfred founded it'. 'Very well, sir', said the Examiner, 'you are competent for your degree.'[2]

Little more than a ritual performance was demanded of the student, 'so futile and absurd', declared Knox, 'as to deserve not only the severity of censure but the utmost poignancy of ridicule'.[3] Nevertheless, as recent historians have discovered, the universities continued despite the system to produce a number of able, learned, well read men, in whom curiosity and conscience took over in the absence of formal compulsion to study.[4]

But the universities were concerned about their 'public face'. Gradually throughout the later years of the eighteenth century they began to recharge the examination system which had been the focal point of so much of the criticism directed at them. Nevertheless, reform, gradual at Cambridge and rather more sudden at Oxford, was not accompanied by any significant change in the scope of university studies. Despite the creation of a more obvious competitive ethos, the choice of texts, the style of teaching and student attitudes remained substantially unrevised. The reforms were simply a positive restatement of traditional methods which enacted a basic minimum standard of attainment from all undergraduates reading for a degree.

The reforms attracted interest and no little criticism, particularly of Oxford, where the introduction of Responsions in 1808 prompted the Edinburgh Review to question publicly the scope and purpose of an English university education. The Review did not dispute that classics, divinity, and mathematics were valuable instruments of education. But that they should be the only subjects of study was scandalous. Oxford and Cambridge were openly maintaining an outdated, outmoded curriculum that was little more than a minor adaptation of the Laudian and Elizabethan codes. The universities seemed torn between the ideas of educating 'gentlemen' for social reasons, and of providing a rigorous academic training. The very purpose of an English university education was vague. It lacked clear definition. The Edinburgh Review provided one.[5]

Influenced by the teaching of Dugald Stewart, the Review called on the English universities to prepare their alumni more actively for the pressures and problems of the nineteenth century.[6] In a rapidly changing world it was vital that the citizen understood the social, economic and political forces at work around him. To the Reviewers knowledge was power and the key to constructive social action. A

man must be equipped with a stock of cultural information, possession of which would enable him directly to influence his surroundings. The means to this end lay not in the study of dead languages or
outmoded mathematics but in a curriculum restructured to encompass the developing technologies of an expanding, diversifying
society – geography, political economy, natural science, commerce,
law and modern history.

Cogent, persuasive, direct and to the point, the arguments put by
the *Review* left the onus on the universities to justify their position.
This they did. The early nineteenth-century ethos of university study
as mental training was developed and articulated in direct response
to the challenge laid down by the *Edinburgh Review*. The concept of a
'liberal education' is in origin defensive, that is to say, it was conceived as an *ex post facto* justification of the *status quo*, developed and
expressed as a counter to external criticism. Furthermore the theory
of the value and function of higher education which emerged was
holistic. It was more than a statement of specified ends. Expressly by
defining the importance of the subjects to be studied and the right
method of teaching them, it related the ends of higher education to
the means by which they were to be achieved. The ends of higher
education postulated by Bishop Copleston were in deliberate and
direct contrast to those offered by the *Review*, while the means of
achieving them were precisely those embodied in the existing
Oxford curriculum. The theory of the value of a classical education
offered an explanation of educational ends to which the university
had already committed itself.

In upholding the Literae Humaniores against the charge of disuti-
lity, Copleston was aware that the scientific and informative element
in the classics could no longer seriously be defended on the grounds
that it offered the most up-to-date and practical scientific knowledge. He formed his defence accordingly.[7]

In a world grown increasingly mechanistic, in the age of accumulative, acquisitive man, the purpose of the university was to counter
the effects upon the individual of gross materialism. National efficiency had been increased markedly by the application of the principle of the division of labour. But at the cost of human dignity.
Specialisation narrowed the individual's vision until he became 'a
subordinate part of some powerful machinery, useful in its place,

but insignificant and worthless out of it'. But society, and indeed successful business, required more from the individual than simply the exercise of technical skills. Broad liberal sympathies and creative, flexible intelligence were at a premium in a society experiencing radical change and deep social division. Through the teaching of classics – and the same argument was used later for mathematics – the university was aiming not to train its alumni directly for any specific profession but rather to develop an elevated tone and flexible habit of mind which would enable them to carry out with zeal and efficiency 'all the offices, both private and public, of peace and war'. The function of the university was to provide, through the subjects best suited to the task, a cultural education and an exercise in method. It was not the knowledge imparted through the study of classics and mathematics which was valuable but the skills and qualities developed by the subjects themselves.[8]

What made classics and mathematics so valuable a medium in the training of minds? The answer was simple. They were uncongenial, unpleasant and downright difficult. They were conducted in their own mode according to their own stringent rules of procedure. This was their strength. To make progress, basic skills appropriate to that mode – linguistic or notational – must be mastered. There was no shortcut. Greek grammar and mathematical theorems could be acquired only with effort and discipline. Furthermore the syllabus, be it construing texts or solving mathematical problems, involved the constant and methodical application of these basic skills. By requiring the student to adopt skills appropriate to another – alien – mode of experience the curriculum required more effort on his part than could reasonably be elicited from any subject read in English alone. Such subjects, easily digested, simply conveyed information and could readily be crammed for the purposes of examination. Furthermore the traditional studies lent themselves to the catechetical method of instruction practised at the English universities. Active personal contact between student and teacher was held to be a more efficient aid to learning and mental development than the passive receptivity elicited by lectures. Small groups could be arranged according to ability and there was constant contact and feedback between teacher and student. The greater familiarity between the two was expressed by the direct contact of mind with mind. The student's level of ability was raised by the greater intellect and gentle persuasion of his tutor.[9]

Contrary, then, to the views commonly expressed, the idea of the university as an agency for developing minds and of classics and mathematics as the best means of achieving that end did not precede, underlie or lead to the construction of the fixed curriculum, but was developed consciously under pressure in order to bolster it.[10] But if the promotion of the academic ethos as 'mental training' does not explain how the traditional subjects attained their pre-eminence it does go some way to explaining why they maintained it. The idea of a 'liberal education' as mental rather than professional training, and for that reason the proper end of a university education, became canonical. It formed what has been described by Edward Shils as a 'normative tradition'.[11] The idea of a university – the 'academic ethos' – became synonymous with the idea of mental training. The curriculum was cultivated and defended within the matrix of this 'normative tradition' and formed its own series of 'substantive traditions'. In the early years of the nineteenth century the 'substantive traditions' of classics and mathematics, and of personal tuition rather than lectures, were complementary to the 'academic ethos' of a liberal education, but for no greater reason than that the ethos was created in order to protect them. Defenders of the university system inherited a powerful tradition which they had bequeathed themselves. What began as a defence of tradition became, in effect, a traditional defence. It was a strategem brought continually into play throughout the 1820s, and '30s but never to greater effect than in 1848, when the universities were forced by fears of parliamentary intervention to consider expanding the curriculum.

Though discussions of change were prompted by fears of external interference, the practical measures of reform were postulated by small but active groups emergent within the tutorial body. They had little sympathy with those who wished to restructure the curriculum to meet an alternative set of academic values. Most college teachers were happy to define their function as arbiters of intellect and, as their livelihood was invariably bound to the methods inherent in the teaching of classics and mathematics, to subscribe readily to their superiority in this respect. They aimed simply to make the system of teaching more efficient by removing from it certain iniquities which had become apparent in the 1830's as the unexpected side effects of efforts to strengthen the competitive ethos.

Fortified by a strong justification of the curriculum, the universities had been content simply to refine the machinery of examination. To have only one test of knowledge and ability, and that at the end of a course, seemed inefficient. It was too great a temptation to idleness. It encouraged too many undergraduates to neglect serious study until the weeks immediately preceding finals, when the less industrious would seek out a private tutor with whom they would cram the rudiments required for examination. The university authorities adopted the view that more frequent examinations would serve admirably to encourage regular and consistent study. Responsions at Oxford, the Previous Examination at Cambridge, and College Collections held termly at both, soon became a sobering feature of university life. College lectures were developed as the master key to their successful negotiation. Consequently most students – particularly those deficient in schooling – found their time and industry occupied solely by the subjects of the official curriculum.[12] This had two direct effects.

The first and most immediate was to empty the benches at professorial lectures. Chairs had been founded to encourage interest in developing studies which lay outside the formal curriculum. They played an important part in the intellectual life of the university. The vigour and eminence of many of the professors was considered by defenders of the traditional studies largely to offset criticism that the university did not recognise new and important areas of science and learning.[13] At Oxford and Cambridge the student was in receipt of the best possible mental training and was also able to attend lectures in history, political economy, law, languages and natural sciences which would keep him up to date with the latest developments in these areas. But, with the arrival of compulsory college lectures, students simply did not have time for anything much outside the prescribed course of study. Even the most popular professors were left without an audience.[14]

Opinion ran high. The university was now more vulnerable to the charge of narrowness. While the status of subjects like history and chemistry was growing nationally, a fixed and immovable examination system had removed all opportunity to profit from them. Furthermore, by removing the professors' audience the universities were seeming to revert to the old vice of sinecure Chairs. They were dispensing stipends while a considerable store of teaching capital lay dormant and untapped.

Second, compulsory college lectures and examinations increased contact between tutor and student and revealed clearly to the former that, while the fixed curriculum conferred undoubted benefits on some students, on most it exercised a wholly negative effect. Tutors found the dividing line drawn between two distinct classes of student: those who read for Honours, and those who did not.

Tutors had few worries about the 'reading men'. Honours courses were exacting and stimulating tests of ability. Competition was intense. To secure a good Class, candidates must 'pass through each subject without making on the average more than three or four mistakes'.[15] Success required high levels of intelligence, motivation and effort. The universities were determined to keep it that way. But by rigorously maintaining high academic standards they unwittingly created an unbridgeable cleft in the student body. Less than a third of all undergraduates read for Honours. The rest followed the pass course, and tutors found these, the pollmen, sunk in a mire of apathy.[16]

The problem was easily defined. Disqualified from the Honours course for whatever reason – be it inadequate schooling, lack of natural talent or inclination – the poll man was forced to study the same subjects but at a lower and less interesting level. Jowett and Stanley described the Oxford pass degree as comprising 'a meagre knowledge of divinity, an indifferent acquaintance with three or four volumes of Latin and Greek, a piece of Latin, about two-thirds of Aldrich's *Logic*, or a few books of Euclid'; another as 'four years spent in preparing about fourteen books, only for examination . . . text books read, re-read, digested, worked, got up, until they became part and parcel of the mind'. The situation was much the same at Cambridge, where the poll man sat an amplified version of the Previous Examination. 'Such', said Jowett, 'is the sum and accomplishment of school and college education.' Whatever the pleasures for Socrates under the English university system, the pig would remain perpetually unsatisfied.[17]

Tutors became convinced that the routine of low-level lectures in the traditional subjects could be of little benefit to the man who lacked either the talent or the inclination to pursue his studies enthusiastically. Nor were they convinced that all pass men were incorrigibly dull. 'This inanimate being who sits in your room with vacant stare,' said Jowett and Stanley, 'is not really stupid . . . [but] ten thousand construing lectures in Herodotus will not elicit a ray of intelligence from him.' The problem was simply one of motivation. Undergraduates could not be induced to take any notice of a course which 'neither fully occupies their time, nor gives them any subjects of interest'. Yet it was clear, said Jowett, that 'the stupidest undergraduate in a Livy lecture, will brighten in conversation, if you speak to him of the Revolution in France'. The tutors maintained that a liberal education ought to encourage mental gymnastic. Any system of teaching which did not elicit mental effort could not claim to educate. Such was the pass degree. They called for a broader, student-centred system of study to be developed within the matrix of a traditional liberal education.[18]

The tutors became, in effect, a small but active body of 'conservative reformers'[19] who, while preserving its main features, aimed to rectify what they considered to be serious shortcomings in the system of study and teaching. They initiated and directed the hand of reform, and did so by playing on very real fears of government interference in university affairs.

Criticism of almost all aspects of university life – financial, administrative, moral, religious and academic – had continued unabated since the early years of the century. By the middle 1840s it was becoming clear that the universities' unwillingness to consider any change in government or system of education was regarded less as a sign of strength than of reactionary weakness. William Whewell informed the Cambridge Senate in 1845 that there were:

> tolerably plain indications that the old Universities are not to expect a continuance of the protection they have been accustomed to receive at the hands of Government

and Jowett asked if it was:

> at all probable that we shall be allowed to remain as we are for twenty years longer, the one solitary, exclusive, unnational Corporation – . . . a

place, the studies of which belong to the past, and unfortunately seem to have no power of incorporating new branches of knowledge?[20]

Rumbles in Parliament suggested not. It was assumed that parliamentary intervention would lead to far-reaching radical change. Something had to be done to prevent it. Jowett and Stanley claimed:

> our only defence against attacks from without, is to build up from within, to enlarge our borders that we may increase the number of our friends. . . . Neither Commission nor Committee of Enquiry need have any terror for us, if it could truly be said, 'The University and the Colleges have the will and Power to reform themselves.'[21]

So much was agreed generally. But the problem still remained. What shape would the reforming legislation take?

It would not be fundamental. Both universities were united in 'admitting the superiority of classics and mathematics as the basis of a general education' and, therefore, as indisputably the best means to the true end of a university education. On that they stood their ground. Reform, such as it was, must be conducted within the matrix of the traditional academic ethos. Jowett pointed at the solution. The university could silence its external critics by simply remedying the practical problems that had become evident in the 1830s. The reforms would be a cosmetic exercise, designed to change the face of university studies without disturbing its psyche. The practical legislation that ensued was ingenious.

At Cambridge the Syndicate proposed, and Senate ratified, the creation of two new Triposes. Both the Moral and the Natural Science Triposes were composed of five subjects: modern history, law, jurisprudence, political economy and philosophy in the former; anatomy, botany, chemistry, geology and physiology in the latter. These subjects were those 'for the teaching of which the university already possesses the necessary means', namely disciplines for which there was an endowed professor. It was intended that classes be drawn, 'from those who do not give large attention to mathematics and classics', in this case the poll men. If the reform was a success, then the university would solve all its problems at one stroke. The introduction of ten new subjects would silence external criticism that the university did not show adequate regard for new or useful knowledge, and would do it without incurring extra expense.

The pass men would find something to interest them and the professors would recover their audience.

Nevertheless, there was the problem of ensuring that the traditional idea of a liberal education was preserved. Consisting simply of information, and taught passively by means of lectures, these new subjects did not require real mental effort and could not, therefore, be said to educate. They might be interesting, they might be useful, but they were not the suitable subjects of true academic study. The curricular hegemony of mathematics was retained by an ironic twist of legislation.

After passing the Previous examination students were entitled to read for the Moral and Natural Sciences Tripoes. But their labour would not gain them the Bachelor's degree. That distinction was to remain with students of mathematics alone. Without admitting the candidate to the B.A. degree the two new Triposes lacked prestige and standing. They were in effect postgraduate courses and dependent on the student's own extra resources of time, inclination and money. They were therefore unlikely to attract many candidates or to draw students away from the traditional studies. While the poll men were required to attend the lectures of one professor teaching the new courses, those who were drawn to the Triposes themselves were for the most part reading men seeking to strengthen claims on a college fellowship. Few in number, they completed their studies in under a year. Some in just one term. While the *Church and State Gazette* declared that 'Henceforward Cambridge will cease to contribute to society merely pale and perfect mathematicians' the statute ensured that little changed, save perhaps the colour in graduates' cheeks.[22]

At Oxford the reforms were less reactionary. All candidates for a degree were required to read for one of the new schools. But their second school, be it Mathematics, Natural Science or Law and Modern History, could only be taken after passing satisfactorily a revamped examination in Literae Humaniores, and candidates could not present themselves for that until their fourth year. All students had then further to extend their residence in order to read for a second, less prestigious school, which sought only to compound their financial burdens and proved a great incentive to rendering that study as brief as was possible.

The new disciplines were hardly likely to have far-reaching effects at either university. But they were not intended to do so. They were introduced to take the sting out of external criticism that the university did not teach new or useful knowledge, and to remedy internal rumblings within the existing system. But the reforms were designed to limit their impact and to ensure that they performed a secondary role. The universities took their stand within the academic ethos of a general liberal education, and maintained doggedly the substantive traditions of classics and mathematics. Mr Punch, drunk on the tide of euphoria which greeted the changes at Cambridge, declared:

> Times are changed henceforth, we know; for, from eighteen-forty-nine,
> The sons of Alma Mater must choose a different line.[23]

He was wide of the mark. The line had been stretched, but not very far.

NOTES TO CHAPTER 1

1 In V. H. H. Green, *British Institutions: the Universities* (London, 1969), p. 50.

2 *Report of Her Majesty's Commissioners, appointed to inquire into the State, Discipline, Studies and Revenues of the University and Colleges of Oxford* (London, 1852), p. 59.

3 Green, p. 50.

4 Dame Lucy Sutherland, *The University of Oxford in the Eighteenth Century: a Reconsideration. The James Bryce Memorial Lecture, 18 May 1972* (Oxford, 1973). Peter Slee, ' "A licence to slaughter"; John Haviland and the reform of Cambridge medical education', *Cambridge Medicine*, 1, summer 1981, pp. 46–7. Green, pp. 47–50.

5 See particularly: 'Traité de Méchanique Céleste. Par P. S. La Place', *Edinburgh Review*, No. XXII, vol. XI (1808), 249–84. 'The Oxford Edition of Strabo', *E.R.*, No. XXVIII, vol. XIV (1809), 429–41. 'Essays on professional education by R. Edgeworth', *E.R.*, No. XXIX, vol. XV (1809), 40–53.

6 Collini, Winch and Burrow, *That Noble Science of Politics*, pp. 23–63.

7 Edward Copleston, *A Reply to the Calumnies of the Edinburgh Review against Oxford. Containing an Account of Studies pursued in that University*, second edition (Oxford, 1810).

8 Copleston, p. 108, p. 112.

9 Adam Sedgwick, *A Discourse on the Studies of the University* (1833), with an introduction by Eric Ashby and Mary Anderson (Leicester, 1969), p. 10. J. W. Blakesley, *Where does the Evil Lie? Observations addressed to the Resident Members of the Senate, on the Prevalence of Private Tuition in the University of Cambridge* (London, 1845), p. 36. William Whewell, *Of a Liberal Education in General and with particular reference to the leading studies of the University of Cambridge*, 1 (London, 1845), p. 110.

10 Rothblatt, *Tradition and Change*, McPherson, *Theory of Higher Education*. Martha M. Garland, *Cambridge before Darwin: the Ideal of a Liberal Education, 1800–1860* (Cambridge, 1980).

11 Shils, *Tradition*, p. 182.

12 E. G. W. Bill, *University Reform in Nineteenth Century Oxford: a Study of Henry Halford Vaughan, 1811–1885* (Oxford, 1973), pp. 12–23.

13 Adam Sedgwick, 'Remarks on Mr Beverley's Letter to His Royal Highness, the Duke of Gloucester', in *Reply to Professor Sedgwick's Letter in the "Leeds Mercury"* concerning The.

Present Corrupt State of the University of Cambridge, third edition (London, 1834), pp. 35–9 (36–7).

14   See, for instance, the sad tale of the Regius Professors of Modern History, in K. T. B. Butler, 'A petty Professor of Modern History: William Smyth, 1765–1849', *Cambridge Historical Journal*, IX, No. 2, 1948, pp. 217–38 (229–30). *A Versatile Professor: Reminiscences of the Rev. Edward Nares, D.D.*, ed. G. Cecil White (London, 1903), pp. 239–43.

15   *Report of Her Majesty's Commissioners*, Evidence, p. 293.

16   [Benjamin Jowett and A. P. Stanley], *Suggestions for an Improvement of the Examination Statute* (Oxford, 1848), p. 10.

17   [Jowett and Stanley], pp. 10–11. M. L. Clarke, *Classical Education in Britain, 1500–1900* (Cambridge, 1959), p. 100.

18   [Jowett and Stanley], p. 12.

19   Garland, p. vii.

20   D. A. Winstanley, *Early Victorian Cambridge* (Cambridge, 1940), p. 198. *Life and Letters of Benjamin Jowett*, ed. E. Abbott and L. Campbell (London, 1897), vol. I, letter to Roundell Palmer, 15 Nov, 1847, p. 190.

21   [Jowett and Stanley], pp. 7–8.

22   Cambridge University Library, University Archives, University Papers, 1847–1949, UP 17, No. 840.

23   'The old and the new Cantab', *Punch*, XV, 1848, p. 223.

CHAPTER 2

'No theory to develope'
HISTORY AND THE CURRICULUM

Despite protests that really it was not amenable to academic treatment and therefore not the fit subject of university study history became part of the restructured curriculum at both universities. Powerful arguments had been ranged against it. Some said it could not be considered dispassionately; it excited the emotions, roused prejudice. Others believed it too easy. History, they claimed, 'seems to demand little more than memory' and would lure the idle and the indolent from studies of greater severity and more lasting disciplinary value.[1] But it could not be ignored. 'Historical-mindedness' – an abiding sense of history, a deep, absorbing interest in the past, permeated the Victorian consciousness. Everyone read history. History books were best-sellers. Only fiction took up more space in local libraries, and still history proved the most common and remunerative vehicle of imaginative literature. People talked about history. Knowledge of the past was an essential prerequisite in educated circles. History inspired works of art, influenced architecture and even stimulated taste in clothes. History was in the air. It was part of the atmosphere.[2]

'The Age of History' was conceived in an era of rapid, cataclysmic change. Massive upheavals in industrial and agricultural production, in demographic concentration, in family and class structure and in political orientation drove a wedge between past and present. 'Historical-mindedness' emerged as a powerful force in early and mid-Victorian England because contemporaries felt an ever increasing distance between their own times and those of their forebears. A

strong sense of history was generated by an uncomfortable awareness of change.[3]

Despite the upheavals in the socio-economic fabric of the nation,
Britain had nevertheless retained its political stability. While Europe
was consumed by revolution, English institutions, the constitution,
the system of representative government, survived, indeed
triumphed. The constitution was Britain's lifeline. It anchored the
present firmly to the past. It embodied the guiding, stabilising principles of political life. The process of constitutional development
was dynamic but moved according to its own set of inherent principles. These could be discovered only through historical study. The
study of English political history was didactic, 'no mere amusement',
said Richard Congreve, 'but the solid groundwork for our guidance
as citizens and men'. The Edinburgh Review went further. Every young
man, it said, should know:

> What the constitution of his country really was, how it had grown into its
> present state, – the perils that had threatened it, – the malignity that had
> attacked it, – the courage that had fought for it, and the wisdom that had
> made it great.

History, it claimed, to widespread agreement, formed a body of
socio-political morality which the responsible citizen could ill afford
to misunderstand.[4]

History therefore seemed adequately to fulfil the criteria demanded of a new addition to the curriculum. That there were
reservations about its powers of training the mind did not trouble
the administrators. That was not to be its function. The new subjects
were introduced simply 'to assist the Tutors in making men work; to
assist the Professors in making up a Class . . . and to give their proper
place to studies, which are every year growing in importance'.[5]
History was certainly interesting and stimulating and ought to prove
attractive to the poll man. There were able and enthusiastic professors to teach it. It was a study certainly growing in importance and
one which featured prominently in both 'utilitarian' and 'academic'
plans for revision and extension of the university curriculum.

But one major problem remained. It was a practical problem. The
new subject was intended as a panacea for a series of ills. But on what
basis would it be grounded? What would be taught? Who

would examine? At what level would standards be set? How would the problems of religious and political bias be overcome? Henry Halford Vaughan, Regius Professor of Modern History at Oxford, summed up the difficulties neatly. 'The whole classical system,' he said:

> has been the development of years and years – Details have always been prescribed with more or less rigour by custom – legislation has had existing custom for its basis. But with regard to Modern History and Jurisprudence there is no theory whatsoever in existence. The statute is absolutely creative. There is, at present, no theory to develope – our first want will be order, unity and guidance.[6]

While the universities introduced the new subject in response to a series of internal and external pressures common to them both, the traditions of their own distinctive institutional structures ensured that they sought 'order, unity and guidance' in markedly different ways.[7]

NOTES TO CHAPTER 2

1   Thomas Arnold, *Inaugural Lecture on the Study of Modern History*, December 2nd, 1841 (Oxford, 1841), p. 4.
J. A. Cramer, *An Inaugural Lecture on the Study of Modern History*, 2 March, 1843 (Oxford, 1843), p. 20.
Bodleian Library, G. A. Oxon. C65 (37, 38, 39) (Hints to Members of Convocation on the Second Examination).
2   For history-book sales see Heyck, *The Transformation of Intellectual Life in Victorian England*, p. 35, p. 130. For preoccupation with the past see P. A. Dale, *The Victorian Critic and the Idea of History* (Cambridge, Mass., 1977); R. A. E. Brooks, 'The development of the historical mind', in *The Reinterpretation of Victorian Literature*, ed. J. E. Baker (Princeton, N.J., 1950), pp. 130–53. For art, Roy Strong, *And when did you last see your Father? The Victorian Painter and British History* (London, 1978). For architecture and dress, Richard Jenkyns, *The Victorians and Ancient Greece* (Oxford, 1980).
3   Thomas Carlyle, 'On history', *Fraser's Magazine*, 2, No. 10, 1830, 413–18, and, 'Memoirs of the life of Walter Scott', *London and Westminster Review*, 30, 1838, 293–345.
4   Richard Congreve, *Historical Lectures* (London, 1900), p. 360. 'Essays on a professional education', *E.R.*, XV, 1809, p. 52. 'The Irish and English universities', *Dublin Review*, 1, 1836, 68–100. See also Olive Anderson, 'The political uses of history in mid-nineteenth-century England', *Past and Present*, 36, 1967, 87–105.
5   Bodleian Library, G. A. Oxon. C.65 (43).
6   Bodleian Library, MS. Eng. Lett. d. 440, fols. 28–9, H. H. Vaughan to F. Jeune, January 1850.
7   I have limited my brief discussion of a complex and highly interesting question to the point made time and again by those interested in introducing history to the university curriculum. For an excellent treatment of the whole question of the hold of history on the victorian psyche see Philippa Levine, *The Amateur and the Professional: Antiquarians, Historians and Archaeologists in Victorian England 1838–1886* (Cambridge, 1986), published, sadly, too late for me to make use of it in this book.

CHAPTER 3

'Such facts . . .
as admit of no reasonable doubt'
CAMBRIDGE, 1848–67

Moral philosophy, modern history, general jurisprudence and the laws of England were not conjoined through any firm conception of the basis of a sound moral science. Whewell, chief architect of the Tripos, was candid about this. 'The list of sciences included in this examination,' he said, 'was selected rather as comprising subjects already recognised in the university by the existence of professorships tending to promote their cultivation, than with a view to offering a complete scheme of Moral Sciences.'[1]

The constraints upon the teaching of any subject within the new system were not those of a methodological nature built consciously into the structure of the Tripos itself. In a flysheet circulated to calm fears about the extent to which the new disciplines would intrude upon the real business of the colleges and university Whewell declared that 'The teaching of the Moral and Natural Sciences will be conducted by the Professors, by means of their Lectures and the books which they may recommend'.[2] Created for the professors, the Triposes were to be regulated by them. The professors were the key links in a very short chain of command. The development of history within the Moral Sciences Tripos and the estimation of its value in the process of education were dependent entirely upon the performance of the Regius Professor of Modern History. Appointed to the Chair in 1849 at the age of sixty, James Stephen got rather more than he had bargained for.

Knighted for distinguished service at the bar and as Colonial Under Secretary, Stephen had resigned his government post in 1847 for reasons of ill health. The Chair was a metaphorical gold watch awarded on the basis of long service to his country. That it was the Regius Chair of Modern History was an accident of fate. Stephen himself was rather hoping for the Downing Chair of the Laws of England. Sir James was no less qualified for the history post than any of his predecessors, or indeed either of his immediate successors. But while he expressed few feelings of surprise or inadequacy at his appointment the demands of the office had changed dramatically. No longer was the Regius Professor of Modern History simply to deliver a series of hour-long disquisitions to those free or willing to listen. Almost overnight he became one of five professors charged with developing a new Tripos, and was forced to accept sole responsibility for the presentation of his own subject. Stephen's attempts to establish the study of history in Cambridge were limited in four fundamental ways.[3]

First, it was clear from the outset that Stephen would remain as he began, the only teacher of history in Cambridge. Without the direct pressure of external compulsion colleges were unwilling to assist in providing tutors in the new subjects. W. H. Thompson of Trinity assured the Cambridge Commissioners that his college would most certainly appoint tutors in Moral and Natural Sciences . . . if and when there was sufficient demand to warrant it. But he did not believe that contingency at all likely to arise. Thompson's prophecy was not without considerable grounding in experience, both of students and of college governing bodies. The new examinations lacked prestige. The prospect of medals, prizes and fellowships lay elsewhere. The new Triposes could offer neither student nor college any great standing, while involving both in extra expense. As Trinity was the largest and the richest college in Cambridge, with the highest student intake and the best teaching resources, Thompson's words were ominous.[4]

Gunson, Tutor of Christ's, offered the solution that most Cambridge colleges would of necessity accept. He doubted whether any individual could teach adequately for all branches of the Tripos. There would not be many candidates, and no college could afford to appoint five teachers simply to instruct a tiny handful of students. Clearly, it was only sensible, and frugal, to leave instruction to the professors themselves.[5]

That is indeed what happened. Until 1862, when Venn returned to Caius, J. B. Mayor was the sole college lecturer in Moral Sciences. But St John's appointed Mayor to teach poll men, who since 1848 were required 'to pass the Professorial Examinations as a means of obtaining the ordinary B.A. Degree'. Honours candidates were assumed to be capable of taking care of their own reading. Mayor did not teach all five subjects covered by the Tripos. He specialised in the moral philosophy he had picked up as Second Classic, and spent most of his teaching time guiding the pass men through the philosophical web woven by Whewell's lectures. Accordingly, while St John's offered a prize for the best work by a college man in the Moral Sciences, it was awarded on the basis of his performance in the moral philosophy paper which formed a minor part of college Collections.[6] Immediately, then, the syllabus was limited to what the Regius Professor alone could manage to teach.

The second limitation followed directly from the first. Taught by one man, the syllabus would depend on the professor's knowledge of his subject. Stephen, of course, was not prepared to allude in public to any such constraint. He defended his choice of subject by pointing to a third, equally fundamental problem. Modern history was but one of five subjects to be taught, studied, and got up for the Tripos. As such, he recognised that 'to those who are engaged in our regular course of academic studies, it is impossible to pursue an extensive course of reading in this or any other department' of the Tripos. Furthermore the course, timetabled at a lecture a week, had to be completed within a year. Any such series which attempted to cover 'the whole of the various sequences of political events which have occurred in all of the nations of the civilised world since the subversion of the Roman empire' – that is to say, the whole sweep of modern history as defined by Thomas Arnold – would be superficial, to say the least. And Stephen was as conscious as any other teacher that thoroughness was the essential hallmark of any respectable university subject. He decided, therefore', not ... to lecture in Modern History, in the comprehensive sense of the term', but to choose a period of history which both he and his students could treat in some detail.[7]

Stephen chose to lecture on France. Its geographical location and political relationship with neighbouring States made its development, in his opinion, 'the central history of Europe'. Even then, with only twenty lectures at his disposal, a detailed history of France was clearly beyond the powers of one man. He would have to teach a limited period and treat it thematically. 'My view,' he said:

> is to divide French history into three great Stages:
>
> 1. The growth of what must be called the despotism . . .
> 2. The triumph of the French Monarchy from Henry 4th
>   to Louis 14th.
> 3. Its decline and fall

and he 'would endeavour to distinguish the successive stages of public opinion which one after another exercised the most powerful influence over the State of France'.[8] But these theoretical reasons, offered cheerfully in public, are less convincing than the personal ones prised out of him reluctantly in private.

Whewell wrote to Stephen. He was unhappy with the history syllabus. Would Stephen not consider delivering a lecture course on English history, something of much greater interest to the average poll man? Stephen replied that it was not that he would not consider it, but rather that he could not. Quite simply, the history of France was the only historical subject with which he was even tolerably familiar. Twenty lectures took a lot of filling, and this aspect of the history of France was really the only one which he could manage to treat at all thoroughly. Whewell himself had ordered Stephen to begin lecturing immediately because 'the abandonment [of lectures], even for a single year, would defeat one essential part of the general scheme, and involve the rest in confusion'. Stephen had not the time to prepare a course of lectures on anything other than his own specialism. Necessity made a slave of reason. The choice was not popular. Poll men could hardly be expected to read studies in French, and few English works touched on French history in any detail, a problem which prompted Stephen to publish his lecture course almost on delivery. But the course content was hedged and dictated by a series of structural and personal constraints. Short of dismissing Stephen, little could be done to alter his decision.[9]

The fourth constraint affected the type of examination Stephen could set his students, and it therefore determined the way he taught and his class studied. It was no small problem. History – even, it had to be admitted, the history of France – dealt with controversial things, with politics, religion, morals. It touched nerves, it excited passions, it provoked argument. At Cambridge it was to be taught by one man. And he, said the authorities, was bound to 'deliver, in his public Lectures, a large proportion of the information which he will require in his Examinations'. Now, said one critic, 'suppose . . . the Student should arrive, in the course of his studies, at different conclusions . . . from those held by the Professor – the awkwardness is apparent'.[10]

Stephen was aware of it. He held strong views about the value of historical study, and regarded the lessons of history ultimately as representative of its real worth to society.[11] He also had his own ideas about religion – to which his critic was alluding. For his first lecture he was quick to reassure his class that:

> all public examinations must, as far as possible, point at what is most absolute, definite, and certain in our knowledge. An examination in history should therefore . . . relate far more to such facts . . . as admit of no reasonable doubt; than to any philosophical theories, which, however just or profound, can hardly be exempt from some infusion of error.[12]

Examinations which asked questions 'as admit of no reasonable doubt' were in accordance with the strict notions of thoroughness and objectivity promoted within the academic ethos by the substantive traditions of classics and mathematics. And Stephen's examinations in history certainly demanded strict factual knowledge. Furthermore, Stephen ensured that they complied with university instructions. All the questions could be answered directly from notes taken in his own lectures, or from a diligent reading of the sources he listed there.

The very first Cambridge examination paper in modern history contains fourteen questions on French history, 800–1600.[13] Fourteen questions in four hours. One question every seventeen minutes. A marathon test indeed. But the questions themselves would have caused little disquiet in the well prepared. Question XI, typical of the paper, read:

Between whom was the treaty of Bretigny concluded; what was the date,
and what were the terms of the treaty?

It demands little more than simple factual recall which, if possessed,
can be stated simply and quickly. Only question XIV:

Explain how the Crusades promoted the commerce of France:- the
enfranchisement of the Serfs:- and the diminution of the power of the
feudal lords

appears to require a good deal of thought and pages of detail. It
carried no more marks than other questions and, like them, it had to
be completed in under twenty minutes. But like the others it is a
question to which Stephen's lectures refer directly.[14] Students took
the necessary information from the professor's lectures and, if
diligent, from a brief synthesis of modern writers to whom he
referred, memorised it, and presented it uncritically as fact. The only
way to complete the course was to attend the lectures. The formula
was not uniquely Stephen's. Both Whewell and Pryme printed class
textbooks. Students of the Moral Sciences were tied to a professorial
monopoly in both their lectures and their reading.[15]

The examination in Moral Sciences was, nevertheless, a stiff test.
The candidate was required to have digested a good deal of information across a broad range of disciplines. The regulations, which
stated clearly that 'the merit of the Candidates should be compared
by means of marks; complete answers to each paper being estimated
as worth 100 marks', suggested a test of accuracy, speed and nerve.[16]
Like classics and mathematics, they demanded precision in the
strictest sense of the word. In the traditional disciplines three or four
dropped marks cost a man his First Class. The regulations of the
Moral Sciences Tripos suggested the same stringency, but here the
candidate had to answer almost a hundred questions spread over six
long papers, each of which carried 100 marks. A stiff test indeed. And
a worthy challenge to any reading man. The procedure of examination was certainly arduous.

How did students cope? The answer is, surprisingly well. F. J. A.
Hort describes the ordeal:

It began on Monday, 9–1, with a good paper of Whewell's, which I did
very fairly; 2–6, Pryme's *Political Economy*, of which I thought myself lucky to

do half, as I had spent (irrespective of a chapter or two in the summer) just half an hour upon it. Tuesday, 9–12, Maine, General Jurisprudence, – a capital paper, of which I did about half; 1–4, a detestable mass of bad poetry, puns, and anecdotic gossip, with a screed or two of absurd law, called Laws of England. Wednesday, 9–2, History: Gibbs, corrected by Sir J. Stephen, whereof I did about half. Yesterday, 9–2, General Paper, nominally Holden, but each subject set by its professor. I did all the Moral Philosophy very fully, about half the History and two or three scraps of the other things. . . . I don't know when the lists will be out . . . I am now going to read for the Natural Science Tripos, which I hope I shall be much better prepared for; it comes on 3 March. . . .[17]

Moral philosophy apart, Hort completed just over half the questions on each paper. Nor did he seem overly distressed by the fact. It was little more than he had expected, for, youthful bravado and hyperbole apart, he had spent little time reading for the examination; and most of that had been on moral philosophy, in which he had become interested as a classic, and in preparing himself for prize essays and fellowship examinations.[18] Yet, despite leaving a sizable proportion of the questions untouched, despite the wording of the regulations, despite the claims of thoroughness and objectivity, Hort took a First Class. How was this possible? Hort scored 96% in his philosophy paper, a mark not possible in the others, which he did not complete. Yet Holden, examiner of the general paper, said that Hort's work bore the stamp of a First Class man, and that, however large the number of candidates, his examination papers were worthy of the highest honours. It was Hort's 'style, not so much of composition as of treatment', which had gained the Class.[19]

Whatever the criteria for adjudging classes in the new disciplines – and evidence suggests strongly that subjectivity and overall impression played a strong part in it[20] – clearly the standards were by no means as stringent as those established in the mathematical Tripos. This was to prove a real handicap to the new subjects, and it hindered their development considerably for a number of years.

The first real estimation of the worth of the Moral Sciences was revealed candidly in 1854. An effort by the advocates of classical studies to free their own well established discipline from the compulsory requirements of mathematics was extended to include the two new Triposes. The measure was destined to fail from the outset. Tradition, conservatism and the academic ethos were against it. The twin Triposes were just three years old. Whewell, their paternal guardian, declared solemnly that:

> It has always hitherto been held as wise, by all who have looked upon themselves as permanent guardians of the interests of the University and of University Education, to innovate slowly, and to treat with great regard existing systems.[21]

The Moral and Natural Sciences must be proved to maintain the highest academic standards before being admitted to full academic status and a significant place in that system. And who better to denounce their fitness than F. J. A. Hort, who had taken a First Class in both? He reminded Senate that 'the primary function of the University is neither the encouragement of the Sciences, nor the bestowal of rewards . . . but education'. The new Triposes were poor subjects of education, for they did not call into play any great powers of mind, accuracy or thoroughness. They consisted 'for the most part of information, and involve the exercise of few faculties but memory'. It was classics and mathematics which alone could give 'real mastery over the facts of *any* Science and security against the intellectual snares of popular superficiality', and they alone which could truly be said to educate.[22]

Hort's contention that it was fundamental deficiencies inherent in their very substance as academic subjects that rendered standards in the Moral and Natural Sciences low, and therefore disqualified them from any serious consideration as suitable vehicles of a university education, held considerable sway in Cambridge. But gradually it came to be challenged.

Those who challenged it postulated a basic revision of the traditional, holistic view of a liberal education. They did not seek to undermine the academic ethos. They continued steadfastly to uphold the view that the university's supreme function was to train minds. What they attacked was the long-standing defensive idea that only classics and mathematics could do it thoroughly. In effect they drew a distinction between the *means* and the *ends* inherent in the traditional view of higher education. The ends of education were to remain the same; they sought to broaden and multiply the means to those ends. They approached the problem in two ways.

The first was familiar. There could, it was argued, be no improvement in a student's mental powers if he could not be induced to work. So much had been agreed in 1848. Clearly, if the student was not interested in, or not particularly able at, classics or mathematics, then he would expend only a limited amount of energy in pursuing them, and his mental development would suffer accordingly. But, said W. H. Drosier, a medical lecturer at Gonville and Caius College, 'different persons had different talents of different kinds: a person of distinguished abilities in Classics might not be able to master elementary Mathematics, and vice versa'. Did that make him any the less intelligent? Drosier thought not. 'Why', he continued, 'should not a person who was not fitted for either Classics or Mathematics have the chance of displaying his abilities in other subjects?'[23]

The answer to that seemed obvious. Had not Hort provided it? Other subjects clearly did not stretch the mind. They were simply stores of information. As such they could not claim to educate and therefore ought not to expect to confer degree status. It was against this argument that the second thrust of the challenge was directed.

True enough, standards were low in the new Triposes, and the teaching left much to be desired. But this was less a function of the subjects themselves than of the structural constraints within which they were hedged. Most students could afford to spend only one year preparing for the Moral and Natural Sciences, and that year was often host to innumerable other scholarly projects. Teaching and study time was therefore short. Furthermore the Triposes were overburdened. There were too many subjects, and the knowledge required of each was too comprehensive. Stephen agreed wholeheartedly with this last sentiment. He told Whewell that he had spent some fourteen years studying the laws of England but, 'looking at the questions proposed in that subject, I must honestly avow my inability to judge whether A has resolved them more accurately than B'. The general paper left him breathless. 'What mortal man could answer those 25 questions, or the greater part of them, without any notice to prepare for them?' he asked. 'I am convinced that they would baffle Hallam, or Grote, or Macaulay if any of them were taken unawares by them.' Standards were low because the Tripos made unreasonable demands on teachers and students, and in doing so it tended towards 'substituting a shabby plausibility for sound knowledge'. Stephen's answer to the problem was clear. 'Each candidate for distinction in the Moral Sciences' should be 'permitted to choose some one such science to which alone his examination was to be confined'. It was the first call in Cambridge for an independent school of history.[24]

Drosier agreed with these principles. He was adamant that mathematics and classics did not have a monopoly of educative technique. He cited his own speciality as an example. The student of chemistry must master rigid investigative techniques. He must learn a new and difficult nomenclature. Besides strengthening the mind, the methods employed in chemistry brought unimpeachable results, and they offered man an insight into the works of nature; they enlarged his understanding of the world and brought him closer to God. Drosier could see no reason why such a discipline should not be considered 'liberal', nor, if the Previous Examination were maintained, why it should not form part of the curriculum which led to a degree. The best course was for the university to award the new subjects full academic status. That would allow them a proper chance to develop, more students would be attracted, and more time would be available for teaching them. A new, thorough and more systematic syllabus could be devised, and, with greater prestige accruing to them, colleges would appoint tutors in the newer subjects.[25]

The argument came to a head in 1859–60. Whewell had warned that the new Triposes 'must be regarded as having failed, if when they have existed for several years they attract very few competitors'.[26] Judged against this criterion the Moral Sciences Tripos was failure on a grand scale indeed. Between 1851 and 1860 a yearly average of fewer than five students sat the examination. Stephen reflected the frustration felt on the part of the teachers. 'We have this year,' he wrote, 'just three candidates to be examined, and I think five if not six examiners, which is absurd.' The calendar for 1860 reveals starkly that there were 'No Candidates'[27] at all. In their present state the Triposes were hardly worth preserving. They must either be reorganised and placed upon a sounder footing or disbanded. The latter would be a retrograde step. It would reduce the status of the professor and leave the university open to the charge that it ignored the developing disciplines and cared little for the less able student. While detractors maintained steadily that any far-reaching change in the university curriculum was tantamount to:

> abandoning the antient landmarks that hitherto have guided her in pres-
> cribing a course of education which has undoubtedly been successful;
> and launching upon an untried course which would probably fail to lead
> to such excellent results

the argument of Drosier and Humphry won through.[28] On 23 February 1860 the Moral and Natural Sciences gained academic independence.

The move had far-reaching consequences. No longer would the substantive traditions developed within the matrix of 'mental training' emphasise a rigid curriculum compulsory on all. The onus now lay with each student to develop his own talents through a number of optional subjects. The criteria for the developing disciplines was the application of strict method and organisation to raw subject matter. The manner of teaching was still more important than the information conveyed by the subject itself.

But still a problem – and a serious problem – remained. How was the newly formed Board of Moral Sciences to create a scheme of studies that would be at once systematic and close-knit? Evidence had made plain that five subjects could not be studied thoroughly by any one man, let alone an undergraduate with limited time at his disposal. Furthermore the five subjects of the old Tripos had never been intended to form a cohesive, organised, methodical unit.

The board set about its task by excluding from the Tripos 'the Laws of England' and adding to it mental philosophy, logic and political philosophy. To pre-empt cries that, far from streamlining the syllabus, the reorganisation had made it more bulky the subjects were grouped – mental and moral philosophy and logic in one; history and political philosophy, political economy and jurisprudence in the other. Students were required to study one of the two sections.[29]

The grouping of subjects was new and highly interesting. Students were offered a choice. They could study the individual mind, and reason about the roots of human action; or they could study society – its history, government, economy and laws. The two groups did not correspond in method or in outlook and increased suspicion that the Moral Sciences could not be synthesised neatly, and that the Tripos remained rather as it had begun, a home for destitute professors.

The board, however, aimed to increase the level of intellectual cohesion by imposing a curb on professorial autonomy. They framed their own syllabus. While they announced with 'regret that they have not had the assistance of a Professor of Modern History in making these arrangements', they were clearly keen to act without him. Sir James Stephen had proved the perennial stumbling block to unity. He had refused to accept the idea that 'Modern History in a Philosophical Tripos . . . can only be interpreted to mean the Philosophy of History' and refused steadfastly to co-operate with plans to institute a broader course and to teach 'ideas' and 'principles' rather than facts and dates.[30] Stephen had support for his views[31] and the split indicated that, in Cambridge at least, there was not broad agreement on the best means of transforming history into a rigorous educational discipline. But with Stephen retired, soon to die, and a successor as yet unappointed, the board acted quickly to prevent long and acrimonious discussion and to develop a more coherent course. History was paired with political philosophy, and became the text upon which political theory formed a commentary. History was taken to mean the story of constitutional development and the growth of polity; political philosophy was the outcome of inductive reasoning about that process. Political philosophy was the philosophy of history, and its pairing with history in the Moral Sciences Tripos seemed a clear acknowledgement of Stephen's dictum that without a thorough grounding in fact the philosophy of history was 'so much unprofitable dogmatism'. In practice, however, it was not to be so. History was taught neither systematically nor thoroughly.

The list of books recommended to students reveals that the core of the course was a close and accurate study of texts – Plato, Aristotle, Montesquieu, Guizot, Hallam and Brougham. Texts had been prescribed in an effort to escape from heavy reliance on professorial lectures and the charges of spoonfeeding, which, so far removed from traditional forms of study, had been among the strongest criticisms of the old Tripos. But while the regulations called for 'a knowledge of the facts of history as referred to in the speculative works', in practice there was little system about this requirement and there were few questions of any consequence on the examination papers. 'History and Political Philosophy' was predominantly a lopsided study of the latter.[32]

Perhaps a professor committed to the ideals of the Tripos could have held the study together. But the new incumbent of the Regius Chair – and until 1869 the only teacher of history in Cambridge – did little to help. Charles Kingsley had not been consulted about arrangements. Unlike Stephen, little administrative power was vested in him, and he did less to try and secure it. Stephen had organised and delivered his lecture course with a strong grasp of its importance and its limitations. Kingsley appreciated neither. He did not make the Tripos his concern.[33]

There can be little doubt that Kingsley stirred passions in the heart of the multitude who thronged to hear him speak. His lectures stimulated discussion and no little interest.[34] But, entertaining and enlivening as they may have been, Kingsley's lectures were not directed to the syllabus of the Moral Sciences Tripos. While, in defiance of determinist philosophies, Kingsley preached moral lessons from the text of history the Tripos progressed regardless. In 1867, as he lectured on the Congress of Vienna, eight of the twelve questions on the first history paper dealt with Plato and Aristotle, while two of the remaining four tested the candidates' knowledge of the texts themselves. So question 1, typical of most, asked:

> How does Plato in the Republic deal with the subject of the division of labour?

The second paper dealt with a wide geo-chronological range of factual information, while the third concentrated upon modern writers – particularly Guizot and Montesquieu. Students required a guide that Kingsley, as professor, did not provide.

It soon became clear that, despite reorganisation, study for the Tripos was little more demanding, no more thorough and certainly no less a process of cram than it had been in Hort's day. H. M. Gwatkin took a First Class in the reconstituted Tripos with what he termed less than 'eight-months' half work'. He was told that he owed his Class mostly to what he termed his desultory and 'idle history reading; which it therefore stamps as accurate and good'.[35]

The Board of Moral Sciences became concerned about reports that standards in the second group of studies were low, and they called an emergency meeting in November 1866 to discuss the problem.[36] Isaac Todhunter read a paper calling for the removal of history from the Tripos. The paper is lost, but The Conflict of Studies, published some years later, develops the arguments it most probably expressed.

Sordid and overemphasised though they might be, examinations were vital to the health of a university. They were the only objective means by which the diligence of teachers and attention of pupils could be assessed. If examinations were to be a permanent feature of university life, then, clearly, it was 'important to pay some attention to the adaptability of subjects to [their] exigencies'. To this end classics and mathematics were well suited. It was a simple matter in those subjects to check the relative performance of students through the accuracy attained in examination papers. For history, however, accuracy meant testing knowledge of 'dates and striking obvious events', so much so that 'the mere receptivity of the student is all that can be tested, to the exclusion of the faculties of comparison and of judgement'. He did not deny that history was 'important and instructive'; it simply could not be organised for the purposes of mental training.[37] Following the paper F. D. Maurice, Whewell's successor as Knightbridge Professor of Moral Philosophy, proposed the motion that 'History . . . be struck out'. The board drew up a report accordingly. In it they stated that 'the papers in history have proved the least satisfactory portion of the examination, the subject being too extensive to be properly dealt with as a subordinate branch of the Moral Sciences Tripos'. On 28 March 1867 history was ejected from the syllabus, and was therefore no longer a part of the Cambridge curriculum.[38]

NOTES TO CHAPTER 3

1   W. Whewell, Of a Liberal Education in General, and with especial Reference to the University of Cambridge, vol. II (London, 1850), p. 44.

2   C.U.L., U.A.U.P. 17, No. 828, 26 October 1848.

3   For Stephen see C. E. Stephen, The Right Honourable Sir James Stephen: Letters with Biographical Notes (private printing, 1906); Leslie Stephen, The Life of Sir James Fitzjames Stephen (London, 1895), pp. 89–90.

4   Report of the Commissioners appointed to inquire into the State, Discipline, Studies and Revenues of the University and Colleges of Cambridge (1852–53), Evidence, p. 197.

5   Report, Evidence, p. 164.
6   St John's College, Cambridge, Archives, Conclusion Book, 1846–72, Min. 8 July 1853, Cl.7, min. June 9, 1858.
7   Sir James Stephen, Lectures on the History of France [in two volumes] (London, 1851) vol. I, p. 5. Trinity College, Cambridge, Add. MS. a.212 (fol. 181).
8   T.C.C., Add. MS. a.212, fol. 181.
9   Sir James Stephen, Lectures on the History of France, vol. I, p. vi, pp. xi–xiv. T.C.C., Add MS. a.212, fol.188.
10   C.U.L., U.A.U.P. 13, 'The Professorial Condition for Degrees', 1851. C.U.L. U.A.U.P. 17, No. 917, 'The New Triposes'.
11   For Stephen's views on history see: J. Stephen, Lectures on the History of France, vol. I, p. 3. C. E. Stephen, Sir James Stephen, p. 155 (Stephen to Wilson, 18 April 1852). C.U.L., Add. 788 II, Papers of Sir J. Stephen. A highly entertaining but uncatalogued correspondence and a draft MS. of an unpublished life of Stephen by Miss Martin.
12   Stephen, Lectures on the History of France, vol. I, pp. 3–4. Stephen was not alone in this belief. See Whewell, Of a Liberal Education, p. 227.
13   The Cambridge University Calendar for the Year 1851, pp. 406–7.
14   Calendar, III; see Stephen, Lectures, I, pp. 109–12. Question V, pp. 145–83, Question VI, pp. 193–4, p. 253. Question IX, pp. 419–33, Question XII, pp. 357–60, Question XII, pp. 259–311. Question XIV, pp. 154–259. For Question 1 see Stephen's advice, Lectures, I, p. 14.
15   W. Whewell, The Elements of Morality (London, 1845) (3rd ed., 1854). G. Pryme, A Syllabus of a Course of Lectures on the Principles of Political Economy (London, 1816) (3rd ed., 1852).
16   Calendar, 1851 p. 26, sections 6 and 8.
17   A. F. Hort, Life and Letters of F. J. A. Hort (London, 1896), vol. 1, p. 180, Hort to Ellerton, 7 February 1851.
18   Hort, Life and Letters, p. 131, p. 145. Hort was a figure of some repute in Cambridge. Third Classic, he took Firsts in both Moral and Natural Sciences, and in the Certificate in Theology. Only a severe attack of scarlatina prevented him taking high honours in Mathematics.
19   Hort, Life and Letters, p. 182–3 (183).
20   T.C.C., Add. MS. a.212, fols. 193–4.
21   C.U.L., U.A. Synd. No. 1. University Studies Syndicate No. 42, p. 2. W. Whewell, 'Remarks on the Proposal, that an ordinary degree of B.A. shall be given on the ground of an Examination in Classics without requiring any other Examination except the Previous Examination'.
22   C.U.L., U.A.U.P., 21, No. 79, pp. 1–4.
23   W. H. Drosier, Remarks on the New Regulations recommended by the Syndicate of 27 October, 1859 for the Moral and Natural Sciences Examinations (Cambridge, 1860), p. 2. C.U.L., U.A., C.U.R. 28.8, fol. 9, (00).
24   T.C.C., Add. MS. a.212, fol. 192–4. Stephen, Lectures on the History of France, vol. I, pp. x–xi.
25   Drosier, Remarks, pp. 2–4.
26   Whewell, Of a Liberal Education, II, p. 23.
27   C.U.L., C.U., Add. 7888, Box 2, Book 111/13, p. 37. Calendar, 1868, pp. 155–8. Between 1851 and 1860 fifty-two men read Moral Sciences.
28   Drosier, p. 2.
29   Calendar, 1862, pp. 25–7.
30   T.C.C., Add. MS. a.212, fol. 187. J. B. Mayor, Remarks on the Proposal to grant the Degree of B.A. to persons who have obtained Honours in the Moral Sciences Tripos (Cambridge, 1860), p. 5.
31   C.U.L., Cam. C.860, 32, John Grote – untitled paper, 25 May 1860, p. 3, p. 7.
32   C.U.L., U.A. Min.VI, 10. Board of Moral Sciences Studies (Minutes), 1860–88, p. 6.
33   On Kingsley see Owen Chadwick, 'Charles Kingsley at Cambridge', Historical

Journal, XVIII, 1975, 303–25.

34   Max Müller, preface to C. Kingsley, *The Roman and the Teuton* (London, 1864) (new ed, London, 1877), pp. x–xii.

35   Emmanuel College, Cambridge, H. M. Gwatkin Papers, col. 9, 39(d), No. 478; col. 9, 39 (c), No. 358. See also Peter Slee, 'The H. M. Gwatkin papers', *Proceedings of the Cambridge Bibliographical Society*, VIII, December 1982, pp. 279–83.

36   C.U.L., U.A., Min. V. 10, pp. 11–12.

37   Isaac Todhunter, *The Conflict of Studies and other Essays* (London, 1873), pp. 6–10.

38   C.U.L., U.A., Min. V. 10.

CHAPTER 4

'A thorough knowledge of books'
OXFORD, 1848-67

The subjects comprising the fourth School, its syllabus and indeed
the methods by which it was to be taught and studied were the cause
of some little concern in Oxford and became the focus of two years'
fierce debate.[1] The School's final form, promulgated by statute on 23
April 1850, was shaped by the interplay of four converging forces:
necessity, convenience, coherence and utility.

Few in Oxford doubted the necessity of establishing new examination Schools. They were the most vital ploy in a stratagem
intended to disarm criticism and forestall external interference in
university affairs. Most agreed that they should comprise 'useful'
developing subjects which for the sake of convenience were already
represented in the university by existing Chairs. But which subjects
were suitable? At Oxford, unlike Cambridge, great concern was
voiced about the intellectual coherence of the new Schools. In this
respect Mathematics and Natural Science caused little trouble. The
problem lay with the fourth, 'modern', school. Numerous combina-
tions of subjects were proposed and then rejected because they
appeared to be little more than 'odds and ends swept together "for
no better reason than that there was no room for them elsewhere." '[2]

Convocation was agreed that the new subjects had little educational value. They were not suitable media for developing the

mind. Their worth lay in the stimulating information they conveyed.
Intellectual coherence was therefore sought in subject matter. The
fourth School was to comprise modern history, law and political
economy – subjects with a common basis in the study of political
phenomena, and all deemed useful to future citizens, legislators and
landowners.

But one further problem remained. How would the subjects be
organised? On what basis would teaching and study be
grounded? The legislators looked to tradition as a guiding precedent. Like the Literae Humaniores, law and modern history were
to be taught and studied through the medium of set texts. This
blunted a series of objections that had been levelled against the
introduction of history into the Oxford curriculum.

First, some had claimed that it was impossible to study a subject so
large as modern history, even if it was confined to Britain and
Europe. But to commit students to a round of textual study served
admirably to delimit a potentially endless field of detail. Oxford
history was made manageable by confining it to what was contained
between the covers of a dozen books.[3]

The choice of books varied a little throughout the 1850s, but for
the purposes of examination candidates exhibited little deviation
around a standard mean of historical classics. The Oxford University
calendar for the year 1859 enters into exceptional detail over the
constitution of the school and demonstrates clearly the emphasis on
mastering books rather than periods. The calendar reads:

Candidates for the higher Classes in Modern History may be expected to
offer for Examination:

Either   (First Period.)

Necessary   { History of England to the Accession of Henry VIII
                { Hallam, *Middle Ages*

And any three more of the following works:-

(1) Gibbon – Chapters equalling in extent 2 vols. . . ., especially c. 38. 44.
     45. 49. 50. 55. 56. 58. 59. 68. 69. 70.
(2) Guizot – History of Civilisation in France.

(3) Sismondi – Histoire des Français, from Hugh Capet (987) to the death of Louis XI (1483).

This may be divided into three periods, each of which may be taken in separately as one work:-

(4)(1) To the death of Louis VIII.
  (2) To the death of John.
(5)(3) To the death of Louis XI.
(6)   William of Malmesbury – Gesta Regum Anglorum B. III., IV., V., and Historia Novella.
(7)   Parts of Milman's Latin Christianity, e.g., the period from Gregory VII. to Innocent III., or the rest of Volumes IV. and V., or Vol. VI. Only one of these periods to count as a book.

The calendar enters into similar detail for the second period, and also for the special subjects introduced in 1854 to encourage close study of 'some original authorities'. Again the phraseology is instructive. With regard to the special subjects:

(a) The time of Charlemagne – to be studied in Eginhard's Life and Annals, and Guizot's Civilisation in France.
(b) The period of the Norman Conquest . . . in the Saxon Chronicle and Florence of Worcester.[3]

Soon the choice of books became standardised. Candidates generally drew from a narrow selection, chosen for ease of prose or simply tutorial expertise. The calendar for 1864 specifies that:

The books in History commonly brought in by Candidates for Honours are these:-
for the First Period: Lingard's History of England; Hallam's Middle Ages; Gibbon from ch. 38.; Milman's Latin Christianity, Gregory VII – Innocent III, with Book XIV. Candidates for the highest Honours are expected also to bring in two of the three following original authors, Philip de Commines, Joinville, William of Malmesbury; studying them minutely. . . .[4]

Second, the study of 'books' was an effective counter for those who believed that history could not be 'dispassionately considered'. Such views were represented eloquently by J. A. Froude.

The problem, said Froude, was that history had become a political weapon. It was fuel to political and religious dispute. History was manipulated to support any point of issue between warring factions. The Conquest, the Civil War, the Glorious Revolution – all important junctures in English history – were battlegrounds of controversy. 'What,' Froude asked, 'is to become of the poor students . . . if their notions of history are to sway this way or that way, according to the majorities in the House of Commons?'

But whereas some maintained that such difficulties must surely disqualify history from all serious consideration as an academic subject, Froude disagreed. Students should know something of history, if only as a basis from which to evaluate the claims of political rhetoric. True, every professor, every tutor was potentially the purveyor of bias and base opinion. As such they must be controlled. With this even E. A. Freeman agreed. The answer, said Froude, was set texts. If they could not completely 'prevent difference of opinion' they could 'limit, to some extent at least, the effect of such difference upon the teaching, and coerce the character of what is learnt into some kind of consistency'. By basing teaching on the diligent study of 'books' the university would create an 'authority which shall control professors, tutors, students, all alike', and a body of information which none could, 'be at liberty to set aside', something concrete which 'students shall definitely learn, the tutors definitely teach, and professors' lectures assume'. The study of texts would put an end to the 'idle' often pointed speculation to which modern studies seemed specially prone.[5]

It was a solution which the Oxford examiners readily adopted. History examination papers were arranged according to the geo-chronological scope of the texts. So in 1853 the classman who opted to study the first period, from the Conquest to the death of Henry VII, sat four papers. The first, 'Hume, Lingard, Hallam', covered English political history between 1066 and 1509; the second, 'Gibbon, Guizot, Hallam', covered the corresponding period of European history. The third was a 'General Paper' asking direct questions of set texts, while the fourth comprised essay questions demanding a broad knowledge of English history from the Conquest to the reign of Queen Victoria. This format was repeated for the second period.[6]

As with Stephen's papers at Cambridge, the questions were deliberately factual. They avoid any hint of controversy by calling for simple statements of fact. They fall into two distinct categories. The first ask direct questions of a particular text;

> By what proofs does Lingard justify the claims of Edward I to be Lord Superior of Scotland? Give analogous cases of Feudal Supremacy over a Kingdom.

The second demand explicit factual recall:

> What Institutions as to the administration of Justice were established by Henry II, or existed in his time?

> Give a sketch of the social and political history of Ireland in the 12th century. What was the immediate cause of Henry II's invasion?'[7]

Both species of question are related. Evidence required for the second would be drawn direct from the texts themselves. So it was that in 1853 the general paper set for candidates examined on the second period draws on knowledge of Robertson's *Charles V* and Ranke's *Popes*. Nine questions are listed. The last two test knowledge of chronology and geography, but answers to the previous seven questions can be drawn direct from the texts themselves. So question (1):

> What were, according to Ranke, the distinct characteristics of Papal policy (1) in its relation with the German Emperors, (2) in the 14th century, (3) in the latter part of the 15th? Mention some important event characteristic of their policy in each of these periods

can be tackled by reading Ranke's *Popes*, volume I (translated by Sara Austin, second edition, London, 1841) from p. 22 to p. 42. Question (3) on the same paper comprises a series of quotations drawn from pp. 290–3 of the same volume. The other questions may be answered accordingly.[8]

The questions demand precise answers. One private tutor warned his students that:

> it may be safely asserted that a First Class is seldom, if ever, gained nowadays without accounting for a very decided majority of the whole number of questions. A great deal of pains expended on only half the Paper will be considered as evidence of ignorance concerning the rest.

The examiners wanted facts, nothing more. The greater number of questions answered correctly, the higher the mark. There was no room for 'opinion'. The tutor advised his students that, as their goal was to complete every question, they should not waste time by reading the paper through but should begin writing immediately. They should write quickly and avoid thinking too deeply about the questions.[9]

If students were left with any doubt as to the value of this advice the answer sheets would soon have resolved them. To consult the examination papers tackled by Oxford undergraduates on hot summer mornings throughout the 1850s is instructive. On pale blue paper of quarto size, the questions were printed with a two-inch space between. It was there that answers to questions like:

> Shew what was, at the time of Charles I, the social position and impor-
> tance, and also the prevailing temper of the County gentlemen, more
> especially in their relations to the Nobility. Trace their progress from the
> time of Henry VII to that of Charles I.

were to be entered.[10] Direct factual answers from unimpeachable authorities certainly reduced the likelihood of bias intruding between tutor and student. They banished any temptation to indulge in unscholarly flights of fancy and imagination. And, further, they made it plain that precision was a virtue actively to be encouraged. The Oxford history student learned early that prolixity was by no means an acceptable by-product of the recently discovered faculty of English composition.

Finally, the study of texts helped overcome one pressing practical problem. Like their Cambridge counterparts, Oxford colleges were reluctant to appoint specialist teachers in the new subjects. But it was made clear from the outset that, for law and modern history at least, such appointments would hardly be necessary. The Regius Professor explained that:

> The tutors have given instruction in the history of the Old Testament and
> in Ancient History, and therefore . . . they can do so in regard to Modern
> History. In all there are textbooks on which the tutors can catechise and
> comment.[11]

Colleges could do one of two things. They could direct their own tutors to teach the subjects of the new School, or they could turn their students out to private tutors who, given the precarious hand-to-mouth nature of their existence, would doubtless adapt readily to meet the new circumstances.

Most adopted the latter course – some even agreeing to defray part of the expense incurred by students who gained a good Class.[12] Only four colleges offered direct instruction in history, and all initially on a part-time basis.[13] Exeter, for instance, organised a system of team teaching. The Sub-rector and two assistants covered the course together. And they did it without incurring extra expense. The college had appointed them as teachers of the traditional studies and insisted they deliver their full complement of classical lectures. The tripartite division of labour proved unnecessary, and in the following year the system was streamlined. Full responsibility for history teaching devolved on Charles Boase. But he was not allowed off so lightly. The college caused him to deliver annual lectures on divinity and classical subjects for some ten years more.[14]

Vaughan's prediction was wholly accurate. Tutors – collegiate or private – experienced little difficulty in adapting to the demands of teaching for the new School. And for one simple reason – it was designed so as to ensure that they did not have to change their teaching technique. The books were different, but the approach was the same. Montagu Burrows described it neatly in a tiny manual called *Pass and Class*. His shrewd little book is a pragmatic statement of official rhetoric, a guide to success within a rigid system. It is a statement of fact, without polemic purpose and devoid of reforming intent.

'Thoroughness,' said Burrows, was the key to success at Oxford, and 'a thorough knowledge of books' was 'only to be got in one way, viz. by laborious exercise of thought', which we may translate loosely as memory. But every student could ease his burden by being organised. The best method of getting up a book was as simple and straightforward as it was universal. 'Suppose we are reading Thucydides,' explained Burrows:

> A blank book may be provided for this alone, or, if large enough, may take in the whole Greek History course, which will be better still. As soon as the text of each of the author's eight books has been mastered, a short but careful abstract of the contents should be made upon every alternate page of the note-book, leaving room for the dates at the side. The opposite

page should contain, in one column, a second and shorter abstract of the first, – the most prominent facts of all, with the most important dates; the rest of the page should be left for remarks.[15]

This method, coupled with a high degree of motivation, was the chief requisite for success. It was followed by most tutors – as Boase's lecture books bear testimony – and drilled into all students. With technique at a premium, Burrows saw no reason to increase the size of one's college bill by extending residence to read for the optional school. 'The preparation for both of them,' he declared, 'is of a sort which can be steadily and effectually made while the chief attention is given to the more important subject.' Indeed, Burrows maintained that, far from being a chore, study for the fourth school made for 'an agreeable recreation' and was much to be preferred to other less worthy pursuits, like cricket.[16]

In practice, whether they spent their leisure hours reading Gibbon or emulating Grace, most undergraduates did extend residence to prepare for the examination, if only for a month. Most spent longer, and as Creighton, an off-colour Creighton [but Creighton nonetheless], discovered, to do well was no mean feat of memory. He took a Second. The cramming defeated him.[17]

Having first mastered the technique of gutting a book, the second task facing the student was to choose his texts. As a private tutor Burrows found that the pressing need with most men was their 'wish to know what is practically the best list to present to the Examiners, and also what it is best to begin with'. The rationale underlying Burrows's selection is interesting. It soon becomes very clear that the capital letter of the law, as expressed by the statute, did not correspond greatly with the lower-case of practice. While the statute declared that the student must be conversant with 'the facts of Modern History to 1789', Burrows gently assured his pupils that once they had chosen their optional period the facts pertaining to the other need be known 'only incidentally and in a very subordinate degree'.[18]

How, then, did the student go about choosing his special period? In strict accordance with the ultimate aim of passing the examination at the highest level and with the minimum of effort, the determining factor was prior knowledge. But, all things being equal, Burrows advised the earlier course, for 'scarcely one Classman in ten takes up the other'. This was no exaggeration. A perusal of the Oxford examination papers reveals that no papers were set on the second period in 1863 or in 1865, reflecting the fact that students had not notified the proctors of their intention to 'bring up' works pertaining to the early modern era. Burrows gave two other reasons for the choice. Firstly, that without the early period the second was almost unintelligible, and that 'the spirit of historical study acquired in pursuing the earlier course will scarcely fail to lead a man on to complete the later'. This theoretical justification rings hollow in the face of the second, more pragmatic, reason, that the modern period was 'harder to tackle'. The issues involved were more complex; they required more detailed reading. As a result, few college tutors lectured on it.[19]

Hallam and Lingard were compulsory reading for the first period. Burrows then recommended that Gibbon be read from chapter 38, taking up the chapters which the calendar discarded; which would count as two books. Guizot would complete the fifth. This, he noted, was not an entirely satisfactory selection, but it offered the most comprehensive route through the course.

The special subject should be 'got up like the rest, from particular books, only as their range is much more limited, a more minute acquaintance with detail is required'. All involved a similar work load, but Burrows suggested a choice from three – Eginhard, Commines and Sismondi. He noted that, with his simple, plain Latin, Eginhard was perhaps the easiest and safest option. He noted with seeming regret that few candidates took the opportunity to 'get up' Adam Smith. But he accepted the fact philosophically. It was after all a difficult book.[20]

How did the books themselves relate to the examination structure? English history was 'the basis of the whole course'. Those who wished to master it required an accurate acquaintance with the dates of English kings, the major events of their reigns, the leading constitutional features and the basic geography of the British Isles. Knowledge was essentially of political events and centred firmly on the constitution and the sources of royal power. Burrows advocated that when reading his texts the student should divide 'English history into general facts, special constitutional facts, and special ecclesiastical facts', arranging the information by carving it up into

periods. Burrows based his advice upon careful study of the examinations.[21] Thus the English history paper (first period) for 1863
asked:

> What English sovereigns during the Middle Ages died mysteriously?
> Sift the evidence, and balance the probabilities as to the fate of each

and:

> Compare the position of Cnut with that of William the Conqueror.[22]

In this respect the paper was little different from that set ten years
earlier. By 1859, however, there were questions requiring more
discursive treatment, and it was in recognition of this that Burrows
advocated a measure of caution to students reading any one of the
set texts. In so doing he expressed an unconcscious but increasing
awareness of the anomalous situation in which the student reading
modern history was placed.

Gibbon, he stressed, must be read through completely. The dictates of the examination required it. There was a growing feeling
among examiners that Gibbon's ecclesiastical history was neglected
by students, who chose to draw their facts from other works. As a
result the examiners would be sure to emphasise this aspect of
Gibbon in the examination. There was the anomaly. Burrows was
aware that under the light of recent research Gibbon's treatment of
ecclesiastical history was defective. But the dictates of the Schools
meant that it had to be 'got up' regardless. All he could suggest was
that students read as a corrective Robertson's *History of the Christian
Church* and Hooker on heresies, fifth book, chapters 51–4; Finlay on
the Byzantines, Hallam on the Mahometan movement, and Freeman on the Saracens. Lingard was more contentious still, but, bar
Hume, his was the only substantial 'authority' which dealt
thoroughly with English history in medieval times. Lingard's
'Romanism' apart, Burrows was only too aware of the problems his
work uncovered. 'The great progress of recent research into this part
of our history', had rendered many details inaccurate. The obvious
answer was, as Burrows noted, to consult the original documents.
But this, he feared, was 'out of the question for most who are
preparing for examination in the Second Final School'.[23]

Here was the rub. Though the study of texts provided a sound basis upon which to rest the School of Modern History, the progress of research had begun to render it inappropriate. As a supporter of the system Burrows had touched briefly upon its weaknesses. Was the classical ideal of scholarship really appropriate to modern history?

Burrows took up the idea again three years later but in a different context. In 1862 he was elected to the newly established Chichele Chair of Modern History, and he used the occasion of his inaugural lecture to deliver a pragmatic reassessment of the role of history in higher education.

Burrows regarded himself as an Oxford historian of the second generation. Arnold was his forebear, a missing link between the primordial days of Nares and Cramer and the bustling world of 'life, energy, progress' over which Burrows himself presided. The early days were those 'of a School which had no traditions' and which, therefore, 'required assistance on the spot'. That was found by basing the school on textual study. It worked well for a while, but at a cost. For it meant that the School of Law and Modern History 'cannot yet have arrived at maturity', and that its achievements were undoubtedly of a 'tentative' nature. Furthermore, Burrows was aware that the School, as it was in 1862, could not develop beyond its present limits. Certainly he quarrelled little with either the chronological or the geographical constraints imposed upon the subject matter, but he was only too conscious of the fact that problems accrued in plenty 'when we come to deal with another principle, borrowed from the customs of the elder schools; viz., that of confining the study by means of the Examinations within the limits of a few authors'.[24] Here was the problem. The History School had existed and functioned without any real regard for the development of historical research. But the publications issuing from that research had rendered what Professor Southern has called a 'ragged, and by 1850 largely antiquated, army',[25] positively prehistoric. Burrows was early in realising that the constraints imposed upon the subject by the theory of a liberal education had confined it unnaturally to the very limited province of a few outdated texts. If history at Oxford was to develop further, then it must take its lead from the progress of historical science.

Herein lay the problem. Burrows's idea invoked 'the controversy

... between the supporters of a general education for all, and those who advocate more or less of special education for each'.[26] Classical studies had been equated with a 'general' or 'liberal' education, while the newer studies had been classed as subjects of a 'special' education. This distinction emerged early in the debate about the scope of higher education and the content of the university curriculum. Those who advocated a more direct correlation between university studies and the world outside were deemed utilitarian. The educational programme which they espoused was more directly vocational than that offered by the universities. They intended to prepare men for specific social tasks. As a result the subjects they proposed were deemed 'special'. The traditional curriculum contrasted markedly with the utilitarian ideal. Its defenders maintained that the university should offer a 'general' education rather than a direct vocational training; that they should develop the mind, rather than prepare the individual for a specific profession.

Initially the distinction seemed sound. At Oxford the classics involved the student in the study of history, philosophy, logic and scholarship. Four separate and distinctly beneficial intellectual exercises. In 1810 no other discipline seemed capable of offering such variety. But the concept of a liberal education was formed as a defensive measure. It was conceived for the protection of the established curriculum. As a result the epithet 'general', which initially was called to distinguish 'liberal' from 'special' or vocational studies, became equated solely with classical or, at Cambridge, more directly with mathematical learning. Consequently any subject which lay outside the established system became 'special' by default. As such, the idea of a 'general' education tied the concept of mental training solely to the traditional subjects. Other disciplines, history and natural sciences in particular, were considered simply to convey information.

By reasoning logically about the anomaly in this distinction, which was drawn between subjects depending upon their place in the curriculum, Burrows was following the trail of the early reformers. Like Vaughan, he was very much in favour of the ends of a liberal education. 'Most practical men,' said he, immediately counting himself among their number, 'have a wholesome dread of superficial smattering. We require thoroughness, depth, solidity. We look to formation of the mind, even in this concluding part of the course, at least as much as to the acquisition of knowledge.' Burrows was aware that, to become accepted widely as a means of education, modern history must prove itself capable of achieving the ends of a liberal education. But he noted further that:

> in this principle on which we should most of us fully agree, lies our greatest difficulty. There is no study in which the consequences of relying on a particular book or a very small set of books are more momentous.[27]

Burrows had hit on a nugget of truth. In stark contrast to its ancient counterpart, modern history lacked concrete authorities. It was a discipline growing rapidly, a mass of developing truths, bitter controversies and conflicting opinions. Truth was a standard to be sought and discovered rather than inherited. This much Froude had realised in 1855, and he had held it as a negative mark against history's educational potential. Burrows disagreed, and in so doing offered an alternative standard by which the value or worth of an educational discipline could be judged. He claimed that the fact that reading history involved making decisions, the fact that it required judgement on the part of the student, was a point in its favour. Reflecting further, he pronounced that 'to form the judicial mind for the purpose of dealing in the best manner with all the problems of thought and practical life is the principal object of all education'. This was no novel view, but simply a statement of the ideal of a liberal education. Burrows divorced the ends of that theory from the traditional means of achieving it. He believed that, were the Oxford history curriculum to be reorganised, history could offer a new and stimulating means of attaining the true ends of a university education.

> The result which a course worthy of this age and place should leave behind it must be something very different from a mere acquaintance with a multitude of facts; it should form habits of systematically organising those facts, of dealing with them accurately, of weighing evidence, of attending to both sides of a question, of patient suspension of judgement where sufficient data are not present, . . .
> The historical spirit must be cultivated as well as the antiquarian, and neither at the expense of the other.[28]

These words are crucial. Burrows was stressing that, rather than being the result of a particular type of subject matter, mental training was the function of methodical study of a systematic and organised discipline. Organisation and method were the crucial factors underlying any viable academic discipline. He was arguing that, far from being simply a mass of facts and dates, history had its own special methods and procedures, and they were thorough and vigorous enough to fulfil the stringent criteria of a liberal education.

Burrows's ideas about the potential educational value of history were shared by teachers of mathematics and natural science. They lent support to a memorial sent to the Hebdomadal Council in 1862. Signed by eighty-three members of Congregation, it complained that the classman's time was broken into by pass examinations in other subsidiary subjects. The constraints of the Oxford system meant that this second examination was too slight to be of any value, yet the classman had still to prepare for some six months in order to pass it and take his degree. This was clearly a substantial drain on financial resources, and it induced many students to read for both Schools simultaneously, causing severe strain and in many cases poor results. If the situation was irritating to the serious student of Literae Humaniores, it was more so to the man interested in one of the newer disciplines. He had first to wade through twelve terms of classical study before being allowed the take-up subject of his choosing. The memorial suggested that if Oxford was seriously to sponsor a full range of subjects they should all be placed on a similar footing and given equal opportunity to develop.[29]

The memorialists won their case. The examination statute of 1864 ensured that, as at Cambridge, some vestige of tradition was retained. Students had still to read for Moderations before progressing to the Final School of their choice. But, as at Cambridge, a new principle in education had been established. While the ends of a higher education remained very much intact, the means to those ends were now widened, potentially to include any subject taught seriously and methodically. The question remained – was history amenable to such treatment?

NOTES TO CHAPTER 4

1   Peter Slee, *History as a Discipline in the Universities of Oxford and Cambridge, 1848–1914* (Cambridge Ph.D. thesis, 1983), pp. 35–46.

2 Bill, University Reform, p. 80.

3 Oxford University Calendar, 1859, pp. 147–8.

4 Calendar, 1864, p. 124.

5 J. A. Froude, 'Suggestions on the best means of teaching English history', in Oxford Essays, 1855 (Oxford, 1855), pp. 47–80 (pp. 62–3). Froude, however, declared that 'All books of Modern History which have been written since the Reformation, have been written in the interest of party, political or theological, in the spirit of principles on which opinions are still divided' (p. 55). The statute book was the only text upon which the School could be based. E. A. Freeman and F. H. Dickinson, Suggestions with regard to certain proposed alterations in the University and Colleges of Oxford (Oxford, 1854), p. 157.

6 Oxford examination papers are of two types – those printed for consultation and those to be written on in the examination itself. The best specimens of the former for 1853–54 are to be found in the collection of Vaughan's papers, Bodleian Library MS. Top Oxon. C 663.

7 Bodleian Library MS. Top Oxon. C 663, Classmen, Period II, qq. 6, 2, 5.

8 W. Robertson, History of the Reign of Charles V with an Account of the Emperor's Life after his Abdication, by W. H. Prescott (London, 1857). L. Ranke, The Ecclesiastical and Political History of the Popes of Rome during the Sixteenth and Seventeenth Centuries, trans. Sarah Austin, (London, 1841). Question 4, from Robertson, pp. 5–6 and p. 71, pp. 161–78. Question 5, from Robertson, p. 385; from Ranke, vol. I, Book III. Question 6, from Ranke, vol. I, p. 135, pp. 137–47. Question 7, from Ranke, pp. 570–74.

9 Montagu Burrows, Pass and Class: an Oxford Guide-book through the Courses of Literae Humaniores, Mathematics, Natural Sciences and Law and Modern History (Oxford, 1860), p. 169. See also F. Harrison, Autobiographic Memoirs vol. 1 (London, 1911), p. 128.

10 Oxford University Examination Papers, 1854. Hallam and Clarendon, 5.

11 Bill, University Reform, p. 256.

12 New College, Oxford, Archives, Motions set before the Stated General Meeting, 1860–66, Min. 14 November 1860. Report of Her Majesty's Commissioners, pp. 216–217.

13 Balliol, Corpus Christi, Exeter, Oriel.

14 Exeter College, Oxford, Archives, College Lectures, 1855–77, C.IV.8.

15 Burrows, Pass and Class, p. 69, pp. 43–4.

16 Burrows, Pass and Class, p. 177, pp. 40–1. Boase's lecture books are the property of Exeter College. JI.1–21. JII. 1–6.

17 Estimates vary wildly. Burrows claimed, in Is Educational Reform required in Oxford and What? (Oxford, 1859), p. 24, that by cramming hard a student could sit the school with simply six weeks' preparation. I find this estimate wildly optimistic. Burrows himself spent four months in preparation for his First – see the splendidly entertaining Autobiography of Montagu Burrows, ed. S. M. Burrows (London, 1908), p. 204. For Creighton see Life and Letters of Mandell Creighton, ed. L. Creighton (London, 1904), vol. I, pp. 41–2.

18 Burrows, Pass and Class, p. 207, p. 205.

19 Burrows, Pass and Class, pp. 205–6. See also Special Report from the Select Committee on the Oxford and Cambridge University Education Bill, 31 July 1867, p. 80, para. 1448.

20 Burrows, Pass and Class, pp. 208–11.

21 Burrows, Pass and Class, pp. 212–18.

22 Oxford University Examination Papers, School of Law and Modern History, 1863.

23 Burrows, Pass and Class, pp. 210–18.

24 Montagu Burrows, Inaugural Lecture delivered October 30th, 1862 (privately printed and circulated), pp. 5–12.

25 R. W. Southern, 'The shape and substance of academic history', in Varieties of History from Voltaire to the Present, ed. Fritz Stern (London, 1970), pp. 403–23 (p. 411).

26 Burrows, Inaugural Lecture, p. 11.

27 Burrows, Inaugural Lecture, pp. 1–12 (p. 12).

28   Burrows, *Inaugural Lecture*, p. 16.

29   Bodleian Library, Oxford University Archives, w.p.   /28.1, Hebdomadal
Council Reports, 1855–65, p. 74. See also *The Oxford Examination Statute [Repeating the
Memorial on which the measure was founded and supporting the statute generally, signed C. W.
Sandford and 82 others]* (Oxford, 1863). and for dissent C. L. Dodgson, *The New Examination
Statute [a letter to the Vice-Chancellor resigning from the Office of Examiner in Mathematics, 2 March,
1864]* (Oxford, 1864).

PART TWO

'A strong and independent position'
HONOURS SCHOOLS OF HISTORY, 1867–95

CHAPTER 5

'Everything depends upon method'
THE HISTORY TRIPOS AT
CAMBRIDGE, 1867–95

The decision to exclude history from the Cambridge curriculum was not popular. True, history as taught by Stephen and Kingsley had not proved a successful element of the Moral Sciences Tripos. But did that really signify that it could not be organised in some other, more appropriate manner? W. B. Warakar asked how Cambridge could contemplate 'the elimination of history altogether' when at Oxford it was clearly flourishing. It was an admission of defeat that academic pride could hardly contemplate, and on 25 November a syndicate to study 'Qua potissimum ratione historiae recentioris et juris gentium studia in Academica promoveri possint' was appointed accordingly.[1]

It was no easy brief. As one of many subjects in the Moral Sciences Tripos history had been allocated little teaching time, and as a result had hardly developed beyond the primitive study of facts and dates. It needed more scope in which to develop. Yet there were grave doubts about the advisability of creating a separate historical Tripos. It would be an unprecedented step. Not even London University had been bold enough to award degrees in history alone. Quite simply, though history was read widely by educated men, still there lurked the suspicion that it was an easy study involving little more than memory. Indeed, the Syndicate concurred in the belief that 'History could hardly be said to constitute a Science', either in method or in the application of its results.[2] Cambridge had no wish to engender controversy. History could not stand alone; it needed 'stiffening' by some more vigorous study. The Syndicate pointed to Oxford as a precedent. Reporting in March 1868, it suggested that History and her fellow castaway Jurisprudence should, with 'various branches of Legal study . . . be made the subjects of a new Tripos, to be called the Law and History Tripos, which shall take the place of the Law Tripos'.[3] In this way history would still be part of the curriculum, but would retain a subordinate position which begged the question of its educational potential, as yet undetermined. The Syndicate simply reorganised the Law Tripos. It now comprised ten papers. Only three were historical.

While the Syndicate used Oxford as a precedent, the Board of Legal Studies denounced the application of case law to their own recently constituted Tripos. In the forefront was Warakar, whose voice had been loudest in securing a Syndicate to discuss the future of historical study. Warakar's response to the report in fact anticipated the discontent which was already brewing in Oxford. He declared the pairing of law with history retrogressive, and detrimental to the development of legal studies. The Law Tripos stood in need of more, not less, law. Despite the ratio of legal to historical papers, Warakar claimed, 'a preponderance had been given to History which there was no right to expect'. He based his claim on educational grounds. 'Law,' he said, 'as a matter of either mental or general training was certainly superior to History, which was a mere effort of memory.' And, if this were of itself not a sufficiently damning indictment of historical study, he added that 'with regard to its intrinsic value: Law was doubtless more useful than History to a man in after life'. Whatever the student's view of the function of higher education, be it faculty development, vocational training or, as Seeley and Sidgwick had suggested in *Essays on a Liberal Education*, a judicious combination of the two, Warakar was sure that history was less valuable than law.[4]

His outburst is readily explicable. He was defending his own newly established Tripos against encroachments which would restrict and further delimit the bounds of its own academic independence. His views about the relationship between law and history are indicative of the attitude denounced by Maitland in his inaugural lecture as Downing Professor of the Laws of England. Lawyers found academic history a time-consuming inconvenience. The only history they required was recorded in the statute book. The history forced upon law students was viewed by Warakar as an unnecessary hinderance. And it proved unworkable in practice.[5]

The inclusion in the Law Tripos of English constitutional and European political history was readily justifiable on theoretical grounds. The two subjects would offer the student the social and political background to the development of English law. But the theory broke down. The two subjects were never streamlined or made compatible with the study of law. They were taught, read, learned and examined in mutual isolation

From the start the joint Tripos was threatened with dissolution. So unworkable did it prove that one prominent member of the university declared that it was hardly worth maintaining simply to safeguard the place of history in the curriculum.[6] After almost twenty years as an integral part of the Moral Sciences Tripos history had been discarded because none of its proponents had been able to adapt a potentially valuable subject matter to the demands of the university system. While many believed history to be an important subject, none had discovered how to translate potential into practical benefit. Now there was talk of its ejection from the curriculum – this time for good. Such was the uncertain position which history held at Cambridge when John Seeley rose to deliver his inaugural lecture to a packed and expectant Senate House in February 1870.

In taking for his subject 'the question of the value of modern history in education' the Regius Professor was under no illusions. He was aware of the poor regard in which history was held at Cambridge. But he well understood the 'causes . . . at work . . . to depress the study of modern history'.[7] They were three. First, the persistence of erroneous notions as to what constituted a proper university education. Second, a surprising unwillingness to build upon what was generally recognised as the most interesting, useful and instructive aspects of history. Third, a marked failure to discover an organising principle around which history could be moulded into a rigorous, viable academic discipline. He addressed the problems accordingly.

The Regius Professor did not expound at any length his views of the proper purpose of higher education. They were already common knowledge. Seeley had been a leading contributor to F. W. Farrar's *Essays on a Liberal Education*, a book which, in its efforts to expose 'the hasty and random way in which the stock arguments' on the subject of a liberal education were 'continually repeated', had caused something of a stir in Cambridge.[8]

Seeley did not deny the importance of training the mind. He repeated the ideas which underlay the expansion of the curriculum in 1860. Any well ordered subject would provide the means necessary to sound mental training. No one subject was inherently more effectual than any other in this respect. And any student who applied himself to his studies in a 'sufficiently liberal spirit' would certainly 'acquire something . . . valuable if not the most valuable thing'.[9]

But this prompted an interesting question. If, subject to their sound organisation, all branches of knowledge were possessed of an inherent disciplinary value, then clearly a 'new obligation' fell upon the student of 'deciding for himself between several courses of study'. Upon what grounds was he to choose? Seeley was adamant. If the means to the ends of a liberal education were to all intents equal, then the worth of discipline must surely hinge upon what Sidgwick had called its 'permanent value' or utility.[10] The student must decide upon the career he wanted to follow and choose his degree course accordingly.

Seeley maintained that every subject, properly taught, developed utilisable skills. Mathematics inculcated precision and lines of formal reasoning. Classics heightened taste and elevated the mind. Natural science brought man closer to nature and to an understanding of the order underlying the universe. But what of history, now threatened with expulsion from the curriculum? Did history really 'recommend itself by less obvious uses'? Were its claims 'less urgent'? Were they perhaps 'obscure, difficult to state or make good?' 'I should,' said Seeley:

> feel embarrassed by the very easiness of my task . . . if I did not remember that after all the claims of History are practically very little admitted, not only in this University, but in English education generally.[11]

He devoted the greater part of his lecture to ascribing a definite function to the study of history, one that could be developed successfully only by a university. The 'school of statesmanship' was not a new idea. But that was part of its strength. Seeley built cleverly on a number of ideas in common currency.

History was held by most educated men to be a vital component in the creation of a critical political awareness. In an increasingly democratic society it was vital that those entrusted with the vote should use it intelligently and responsibly. The citizen must be aware of the political forces at work about him and the nature of the issues confronting him. His political education was best developed by a study of British and European history, from which an understanding of modern society could be drawn. So much had underpinned the addition of history to the university curriculum in 1848. Stubbs had been first to recognise the importance of building on this belief. Like Seeley, Stubbs was acutely aware that as an academic subject history 'needed some vindication as a *bona fide* study, valuable in itself and in its results, before it could be allowed to compete with other older and more organised departments of learning'. He never tired of stressing that history was 'an indispensable requisite for every-day existence in a civilised country'. But for Stubbs the worth of history as 'a tool or a stock of tools capable of employment for ulterior purposes' depended entirely upon its accuracy. Sound reasoning could hardly rest upon false data. For the purposes of accuracy and objectivity the university must house a body of men who would study history 'for its own sake', to add to the 'stock' of facts, an ignorance of which prevented a man from playing the 'humblest part' as a citizen. These men could also develop a syllabus and lead a critical and objective analysis of these facts, free from the distortion of party prejudice. Stubbs suggested that if history were to be valuable in itself then it must be written 'scientifically', that is, objectively, without reference to commercial concerns or to maintaining a particular political view. If history were to provide valuable results, then it must be based on 'scientific', objective study, and read in a critical spirit. Both the production and teaching of scientific history were to be the province of the university.[12]

Seeley extended the idea – an idea he had rejected as impractical some seven years earlier. He agreed that history was an important part of every man's general education. But men ought to be educated directly and specifically for citizenship. The Cambridge history school would offer something unique. It would provide a technical training for apprentice politicians. Combined with political economy, history was to form the sound basis of a rational political science. This was ground surveyed by others.[13] But by suggesting that Cambridge was the natural home of such an undertaking Seeley was making a new claim. The science of politics did not yet exist. It could be nurtured successfuly only by scholars in a scholarly environment.

Both Seeley and Stubbs recognised that history stood low in educational esteem. They both played on the popular belief that history was interesting, but maintained that it could be truly useful only if studied scientifically. The concept of science conferred on history a dignity which raised it above the mere study of facts and dates. Stubbs found science in method, in the systematic and objective search to establish truth. But Stubbs was an accredited historian. In 1870 Seeley was not. He knew no love of history 'for its own sake', and his ideas about education hardly allowed him to encompass it. To have value as a university study, history must be organised in such a way as to confer some benefit to a man in later life. Seeley's science was based on a methodical and systematic organisation of the facts of history to provide a political data base. It was a concept which had another equally important function. Having ascribed to history a definite value in the process of education, the 'school of statesmanship' helped to determine Seeley's solution to the third, equally pressing problem. How was the study of history to be organised and delimited?

It was no small problem. To be acceptable as a university subject, any discipline must be thorough, systematic and methodical. To be manageable it must be limited in scope. Seeley was aware of the difficulties. 'If history were taken to have for its subject matter all that has happened in the world,' he said, then 'it would not be a single science but the inductive basis of all sciences whatever.' But he also had a solution. Just as each branch of the natural sciences claimed for its own a specific province of the physical world, so the study of history should concentrate on a particular class of phenomenon. Historical facts were to be classed according to type. Type was determined with reference to the school's function. The 'school of statesmanship' would develop the scientific study of facts pertaining to the growth of States in the modern world. As a vital component in a new political technology Seeley stressed the importance of studying modern rather than ancient society. Modern history was the direct route to an understanding of, and perhaps even to solving, the problems of the modern world. Ancient history supplied analogies, modern history direct truths.[14]

Seeley's lecture was vitally important. Not so much for the content as for the manner of its delivery. Seeley never attempted, nor ever seriously intended, to develop the model 'school of statesmanship' in Cambridge. It was merely a rhetorical device employed to impress listeners with the importance of developing historical study. Indeed, within ten years Seeley had abandoned even the pretence of creating a school for statesmen. His experience as an historian at the hands of non-specialist reviewers led him, like Stubbs, to stress the importance of a university-based clerisy of historical scholars who would strive to maintain a conceptual hygiene and keep the professional study free from the grip of literary terrorists and editorial desperadoes.[15] The value of Seeley's inaugural lecture was that it gave impetus to historical study in Cambridge.

Seeley's aims were perfectly well understood by his contemporaries. Some, like Thompson, Master of Trinity, did not agree with his overall conception of a university education, and were disturbed by what they heard. But Thompson was Regius Professor of Greek, and from once having been an avid supporter of classical studies Seeley had dismissed them out of hand. W. E. Heitland gauged the general mood of the Senate House. The audience, he said, understood that Seeley was 'a man of ideas, bent upon gaining for the study a strong and independent position'.[16] Within the hour he had reduced history to manageable proportions, invested it with system and method, and imbued the study with a definite value not only to the individual student but also to the nation. Suddenly all things seemed possible. Their success depended now on the university's willingness to make them work. That willingness was put to the test in 1872. On 8 March the Board of Legal and Historical Studies reported that no longer could both subjects be contained suitably within the confines of a single Tripos. The board called for history's expulsion.[17]

There was little doubt that the experiment of bonding law and history had proved a failure. Though no candidates had actually been 'plucked', only one had gained a First Class Honours degree. In a status-conscious environment the failure to produce First Class men reflected badly on the Tripos. Abdy laid the blame squarely on the history teaching. No candidate in any year, he claimed, had consistently secured half marks on all the history papers. The reason, said Latham, Fellow of Trinity Hall, was that no student ever took up law and modern history through an overwhelming interest in the latter. The unsystematic study of disconnected elements of history simply proved an irritant which annoyed and discouraged law students. So unworkable had the joint Tripos proved that E. C. Clark declared it not worth maintaining simply to preserve history's place in the curriculum. A. W. Ward was worried that history might be 'left to itself out in the cold'.[18]

There was little danger of this. Seeley's lecture and 'media' personality had focused attention on the study. The Regius Professor used his position to the full. He:

> quite agreed that it was desirable that there should be a Tripos for Law alone, and that Modern History should be removed out of it . . . but he questioned the desirability of having a Law Tripos alone if History was not likely to be introduced in some other way. On the vain hope that Modern History would have a Tripos of itself he should protest.

Seeley shifted the focus of debate away from a more efficient Law Tripos to the future of his own subject. He maintained that 'whilst they effected a change to improve the study of Laws they should secure the study of history against injury'. If ever there had been a 'tacit understanding' that a curricular niche would be found for History, 'it was not enough to take this for granted'. He:

> therefore suggested the appointment of a syndicate to consider the best means of dividing Law and Modern History; and avert the danger of a year or two – perhaps more – passing between the beginning of a new Law Tripos and the proposed Historical Tripos.[19]

Seeley found support in Henry Sidgwick. Sidgwick declared it his intention to vote against the statute in its present form. He would do so because it made no provision for historical study, a study of great importance. Sidgwick said that he had been a member of the

Syndicate which had united law and modern history in 1867. He explained that then there had 'seemed . . . little chance of the university instituting two new Triposes'. The Law and History Tripos was a compromise reached within narrow institutional limits. Through Seeley's persistence attitudes had now softened. History was clearly worthy of academic independence. It would attract many students from that 'not inconsiderable class who intend to take part in politics and were desirous of some special training'.[20]

The Board of Legal and Historical Studies now had a problem. Having raised the question of separating law from history to the benefit of law, it found that eventuality contingent upon a secure settlement for history. Unless a compromise was reached, clearly the separation could become a long, drawn-out, tedious process. Seeley had played his hand expertly. On 23 May 1872 a Syndicate was appointed to consider the best means of separating the Tripos.

But still the perennial problem persisted. By what means was the subject to be organised and streamlined into a rigorous academic discipline? Seeley and Sidgwick had made their views clear. History was worth studying for the information it conveyed about political behaviour. Political history and political economy should form the basis of the new Tripos. Both names carried weight. Seeley was chief representative of the discipline in Cambridge. Sidgwick had taught history for the Moral Sciences Tripos. Only Basil Hammond, who for the next twelve years clung vainly to the idea that Law and Modern History might yet be saved, had any comparable experience of history teaching. There was one exception: A. W. Ward, Fellow of Peterhouse, and Professor of History and English Language and Literature at the Owens College, Manchester. And he had other ideas. As a non-resident member of the Board of Legal and Historical Studies he could take no real part in Combination Room or Arts School debates. So he wrote, and at length, on the great opportunity that had presented itself to the Syndicate.

Like Seeley, Ward's first aim was to clear history against charges that it was not sufficiently rigorous to be worth studying. Like Seeley he maintained that all subjects could answer the needs of mental discipline. Like Seeley he was aware that many believed, 'to examine a man in History is merely to ascertain whether he had within a given time amassed a certain amount of information – in other words, to set a premium on cram'. It was the old taunt. Like Seeley, Ward dismissed it. 'To these arguments,' he said, 'the answer is that in examination, as in study, everything depends upon method.' Like Seeley, Ward was sure that the secret of academic success was proper organisation of the subject. But here they parted company.

Seeley's ideas about historical study were assembled and pronounced for effect. He had to convince a non-specialist audience – with whom the immediate future of historical study lay – that history really was worth developing in Cambridge. He did so by building on a widespread belief in the value of history and suggesting a systematic treatment of it. Seeley himself was no historian. Ward, however, was. Like Stubbs he believed that 'the historical habit of mind' was a thoroughly admirable educational goal, worthy of attainment and valuable in its own right. The aim of a History Tripos should not be to inculcate the principles of political science but to provide a block of essential cultural information and to encourage powers of criticism and composition; to develop the ability to accumulate, analyse, combine and arrange information in a lucid narrative. An Historical Tripos should therefore comprise two distinct elements: an outline history of the world, combined with the rudiments of the 'cognate sciences' – law, political economy and geography – and, most important, the study in detail of a special historical subject read in the original authorities.

Ward offered an alternative system of study. He believed that history could fulfil the criteria of mental training without reference to crude, directly vocational concerns, and he claimed that its boundaries should be extended beyond the narrow study of political facts. The techniques of historical research were sufficiently rigorous to warrant inclusion in any scheme of higher education.[21]

When the Syndicate reported on 3 December they concurred with the decision of the Board of Legal and Historical Studies that both subjects were too wide-ranging to be coupled in one Tripos. Pressure from Seeley, Sidgwick and Ward had worked. The Syndicate suggested that history 'requires a separate and distinct Examination'. If history was to become an effective educational discipline, then it needed to be placed on a wider basis than Cambridge hitherto had contemplated.[22]

One commentator has made the tempting suggestion that the

practical measures espoused by the Syndicate are expressive of a compromise between the views of Seeley and those of Ward.[23] While tempting, the idea is also misleading. Certainly the Syndicate paid lip service to Ward's plea for measure of continuity in history teaching. Whereas Seeley had denied ancient and medieval history any serviceable educational utility, the Syndicate suggested that the student be familiar with at least a portion of each major chronological division of the subject matter. These portions were also similar in format to Ward's 'special' subjects, for the Syndicate suggested they be studied with reference to the original authorities. But they were broader in extent than those Ward had called for and they were not to be studied in the context of the general period in which they fell. Certainly Ward himself saw no similarity between his proposals and the Syndicate's report.[24]

The chief feature of the scheme, however, was the Syndicate's decision that the study of history be 'accompanied with the chief theoretical studies which find their illustration in history', these being constitutional law, political economy, economic history, international law, jurisprudence and political science. To Ward at least this was a sure sign of Seeley's complicity in drafting the scheme. In one sense it was. Seeley agreed wholeheartedly with the idea of cognate sciences. He had been sure from the start that the prevailing opinion was soundly against studying history alone. Cambridge had never promoted literary study. Even in classics the reading of texts had little place in the Honours curriculum. There were no literary traditions upon which to build. History needed a start, but it could not stand alone; so Seeley stressed the potential importance of history as a data base for political sciences as a widely understood alternative. The Arts School debates bore him out. The prevailing opinion was that by itself history 'would soon degenerate into mere annals'. Basil Hammond maintained firmly that:

> the study of History alone, at least in its earlier stages, has a tendency to exercise too exclusively the memory and receptive imagination of the Student, and to leave comparatively unemployed the higher faculties of apprehending clearly and applying accurately general principles, and handling abstract ideas with ease and precision.

As an unknown quantity in the context of Cambridge studies the university would not sanction the idea of exclusive reliance on history's powers of training the mind. Seeley simply backed and rode the right horse.[25]

But he had little say in the specific subjects of the new Tripos. These were decided by practical considerations beyond his influence. First, history was a new subject. Whatever format was chosen, some distaste would be expressed. The Syndicate looked to tradition for a guiding precedent. Their final decision was, as they revealed in their report:

> in accordance with the arrangement adopted in the reconstitution of the Moral Sciences Tripos in 1860, which was abandoned in a great measure in consequence of the practical difficulties found in working two simultaneous sets of papers.

Dealing with a new and unstable academic mixture, the Syndicate settled, as Oxford had, for a more thorough and exacting restatement of the old order.[26]

The regulations were also drawn up with administrative details in mind. One major practical concern confronting the Syndicate was to keep the Tripos running – to ensure and maintain an adequate supply of teaching in the subjects designated for examination. There were few history teachers in Cambridge. On the foundation of the Law and Modern History Tripos Trinity College had made provision for history teaching, and St John's College appointed a lecturer to instruct in both disciplines. But unlike Oxford, where since 1848 history had been a designated and more prominent part of the curriculum and had acquired status gradually with time, the smaller Cambridge colleges did not respond to the needs of the new discipline. In 1873 Seeley's only endowed colleague was Basil Hammond, who had replaced C. H. Pearson at Trinity. A pure History Tripos was clearly too wide-ranging to be taught by two men.

The practical details of the Tripos were drawn up with this fact in mind. The 'general' periods of ancient, medieval and modern history specified by the board were short enough to be assimilated quickly by lecturers, and they were subsequently chosen in relation to the specialisms of the teaching staff. The 'cognate sciences' were those in which endowed teachers – generally professors – were available to instruct.

Thus it was that Seeley, whose historical knowledge was self-con-
fessedly limited, decided to concentrate his energies on the modern
period, while Hammond specialised in constitutional law and
history. The cognate sciences were covered by lecturers and professors from other disciplines. Fawcett taught political economy and
Stanton economic history. Lawrence of Downing taught law and
general jurisprudence, Sidgwick assisted Seeley with political philosophy, while the Public Orator lectured on the general period of
ancient history. The Tripos had to be planned initially around available resources, and teachers had then to tailor their aspirations to the
dictates of the syllabus. There was little room for experiment, and
resources were insufficient for the board to consider changes. But
the new discipline did offer an opening for ambitious and
determined young men. It further presented colleges with the
opportunity of developing a reputation in a new and expanding
subject. G. W. Prothero and King's College formed one such combination.

Prothero had graduated from King's as sixth Classic in 1872. While
teaching at Eton he became interested in history. A year at Bonn
under Von Sybel confirmed the historical leanings, and Prothero
began to plan for himself a career in history. The time seemed
propitious. Cambridge needed history teachers, and Prothero
himself held a fellowship at King's. He approached Henry Jackson,
Master of Trinity, for advice. Jackson was less than sanguine about
the prospect of a good living from history teaching. But, cautious as
he was, his words were not without hope. Jackson believed the
History Tripos would develop quickly – perhaps more quickly than
any of its rivals. But he doubted that it would attract students of great
promise or high intellect. The best men, he said, 'will be men who
have already graduated in Classics and Mathematics, and they will in
general dispense with teaching in history, except what is given by the
Professor'. Nevertheless 'The subject being virtually a new one, it is
likely that anyone who establishes himself here ... would secure
such teaching as there is to be had'.[27]

This was all the encouragement Prothero needed. He made it clear
to King's that he would attempt to secure the permission of the
History Board to advertise lectures on historical subjects. While he

began clambering to secure the necessary foothold in the administration of the new Tripos, his college debated nervously its own
position in this respect. The question of securing for Prothero an
official position as college lecturer was first raised in Council in
January 1875. It was deferred repeatedly.[28]

Prothero wrote to the board with a proposal to lecture in international law. Seeley responded sensitively. He was keen to build up a
large pool of teachers, but he had to ensure that between them they
covered as wide a range of subjects as was possible. Bryan Walker
lectured upon the subjects in which Prothero had expressed an
interest. But Seeley was aware that Walker was pricing himself out of
the market. The Inter-collegiate Lecture Scheme was as yet in its
infancy, and adopted fully only by the Boards of Classical and Mathematical Study. Unless their colleges had established reciprocal
agreements, students had to pay lecture fees to teachers from
colleges other than their own. History was not well enough established, or popular enough with students, for the wheels of bureau-
cracy yet to have turned this far. It was important that lecturers adjust
their fees accordingly. In Walker's case Seeley recognised that
students were voting with their wallets, and that 'a great interreg-
num' had 'set in'. Prothero he envisaged as 'evidently the Rudolf of
Hapsburg just visible in the distance'. But Prothero must send details
of his courses.[29]

Prothero was encouraged, and wrote once more to Seeley with an
extended list of lecture topics. Seeley was responsive, but suggested
that Prothero modify his plans with the Tripos firmly in mind.
Economy of effort was vital, and Prothero had evidently suggested
lecturing upon a subject that was not part of the Tripos. Seeley
indicated gently that the men would have neither time nor inclination for such a subject. 'It would be a pity,' he said, 'to discourage
yourself by trying to get up a class and failing.'

Seeley approved of Prothero's plan to lecture on the Hohen-
staufen. That was to be a designated general period in 1876. He made
precise suggestions as to the type of lectures which Prothero should
deliver on international law, and to their format and content. Seeley
reassured Prothero that there was no rush to deliver lectures.
Organisation of the Tripos was strict. Students could attend only one
lecture, and concentrate upon one subject at a time. Lecturers had to

fit their subjects neatly within the general administrative framework, which had been designed to ensure that the maximum effect was gained from minimal resources. Seeley was a skilled administrator and a tactful, if self-appointed, departmental head. He told Prothero that a balance between personal enthusiasm for a particular period and the requirements of the Tripos was vital. He was aware that drive, commitment and enthusiasm made for an able and influential teacher, and he stressed that he did not want to ask the young Prothero 'to do anything but follow . . . [his] strongest inclination'. But, for the purposes of historical teaching in the university, it was vital that Prothero direct his own reading to subjects of the curriculum. The professor suggested that the Middle Ages might prove a particularly fruitful area.

Here was Prothero's opportunity. Seeley had stated plainly that Prothero was more than welcome to throw in his lot with the new school. He had expressed a wish that he could 'count on' Prothero 'for the future'. Their visions of the future were very much the same. Seeley had opted to specialise in modern, Hammond in constitutional, history. The classicists covered ancient history. Seeley offered Prothero his own period. As *Simon de Montfort* and *English Constitutional Documents* prove, the dictates of the Tripos shaped historians in more than one way. Necessity proved the most demanding of masters.[30]

King's soon responded to Prothero's newly found role. By agreeing in October 1875 to pay the fees of all out-of-college lectures delivered with respect to a university Tripos, it had made an important concession to students of the less well endowed disciplines. A month later, and after much deliberation, the College Educational Council called

> the attention of the College to the want of teaching in History, suitable to the newly established Historical Tripos. Considering the importance of the subject and the small number of Lectures at present devoted to it throughout the University, the Educational Council think that the College would do well to establish a Lectureship in order to promote the study, and improve the teaching at present provided in that subject.

Motives were mixed. 'This recognition of the subject', the Report continued:

> would be of itself a great advantage, and would prove the willingness of

the College to contribute towards the common wants of other Colleges, the advantage of whose teachings is by means of the Inter Collegiate System, so largely enjoyed by our own students.

In March 1876 Prothero was elected to a lectureship. It was the first sign that the History Tripos would be recognised at last by the colleges. King's, newly reformed and re-oriented, was aiming to play an influential role in university life, and to acquire a reputation for learning and intellectual activity. Prothero was taken up as an investment. King's aimed to do for History what Trinity had done for Moral Science.[31]

They increased their teaching personnel accordingly. In September 1876, swept on a wave of scandal, Oscar Browning returned to his college. King's began, and, for the entire length and breadth of his career, remained, suspicious of the rotund Eton émigré, who had forgotten nothing, and often, it seemed, had learned even less. Proposals to elect him to a lectureship in 1877 were crushed. But whatever the fears and secret revulsions of some King's men, Browning's invitation to lecture was accepted with willingness by the History Board, which took steps to secure his services for an extended period. Browning was to lecture on international law and treaties. The subject was chosen with the Tripos and the teaching resources firmly in view. Now each of the four specialist history teachers covered between them all but one of the four selected periods, and that was the province of the Public Orator. Like Prothero, Browning made a virtue of necessity. In 1880 he was elected to a college lectureship, and, in tandem with Prothero, helped to establish King's in Cambridge, like Balliol in Oxford, as the historical college.[32]

Between them Seeley, Hammond, Prothero, Browning and then Cunningham, who began lecturing for the Tripos in 1879, managed to cover almost every subject in the syllabus. Only political economy remained firmly outside their range, and Fawcett, and then later Marshall, taught that. Nevertheless the rigid division of function imposed upon the lecturers for the greater good of the Tripos caused problems. There was little room for the 'progress' which the board felt the newly found school could make. The university ignored two requests for an increased complement of endowed lecturers who would then 'enable the Historical School to compete,

with a fair chance of success, against the older and more highly
endowed branches of study'.

In 1883 the board announced that 'The provision for University
teaching in History is inadequate and precarious, and imperfectly
organised'. While the subjects of the Tripos were effectively covered
by the teaching staff, lecturers had to teach periods of which they had
little first-hand knowledge. If any lecturer was dismissed from his
college post or otherwise lost to the world, then the whole structure
of teaching could collapse. Furthermore, in lectures pertaining to
the cognate sciences, history students sat with those of other disciplines. The classes were large, and, as such, the 'individual attention
which is required for efficient teaching' was lacking.[33]

In May 1884 the board's pleas were finally heard. The three college
lecturers – Prothero, Hammond and Browning – and the two
unendowed teachers – Thorneley and Cunningham – were offered
university lectureships. The university had obviously decided to
secure the position of the present teaching staff by providing addi-
tional security beyond their college posts, which were held on a
short-term basis. The conditions of tenure are interesting. The
lecturers were not to be subject to the jurisdiction of the Regius
Professor. Nor were their lectures to be compulsory on students.
The university posts were not intended to cut across the traditional
authority of the college tutor who sanctioned the lectures which his
men should attend. The lectureships were simply a convenient
method of ensuring that the inter-collegiate lecture system continued to work; they were a bulwark against the possible dangers of
losing staff.[34]

The appointment of the university lecturers was important in
another less obvious way. The Tripos was administered very firmly
by the board, many members of which had been instrumental in
setting it up. The first ten years had seen a determined effort to
survive and prosper. The creation of the new lecturers was a sign that
the university recognised history as a permanent part of the curriculum. Survival was assured. Now the board could consider more
clearly the lie of the road ahead. It is significant that agitation for
Tripos reform followed very soon after the appointment of the
university lecturers was confirmed, and that its strongest adherents
were two of those lecturers.

What, then, did the reformers react against? How had the practical business of history teaching been reflected in the curriculum? What was required of the Cambridge history student between 1873 and 1884?

The freshman coming up to Cambridge in October 1874 had first to pass his Previous Examination, which, given a grounding in classics and mathematics and a little effort, he would do before Christmas. He had then three years ahead of him. If he chose to read history as the avenue to his BA degree he was faced with a considerable array of subjects – constitutional history, English political history, periods of ancient, medieval and modern history, international law, political philosophy, jurisprudence, economic history and political economy. Where would he begin?

Owing to the paucity of teaching resources, courses were organised rigidly. Teaching for the History Tripos had settled quickly into a regular pattern. Students were designated to attend a particular course or courses in a particular term, every term, for the duration of their studies. A course missed could not be recovered. Students were advised to read for each subject while attending advertised lectures on it. Studies began with English political history and constitutional law and history, reading for which would be completed before the beginning of the second year, when political economy, economic history and one general period would be 'got up', and reading for international law, political philosophy and the second general period would be begun. The final year would be spent completing those subjects, and attending lectures on general jurisprudence and the final general period. Students would sit their examinations in December of the fourth year.[35]

The relationship between reading and lectures is important. Basil Hammond, who acted in a general capacity as adviser to students whose college lacked a history tutor, indicated that a detailed knowledge of the whole subject could not be gathered from lectures alone. For that he must rely on his own reading. Hammond outlined a short list of works from which the student might acquire a 'tolerably complete' knowledge of history. No man, he suggested, could read them all, but every man should endeavour to tackle a good selection, the specific number being determined by the extent of previous reading in the subject. The only advice which Hammond was prepared to offer on reading was that:

> everyone should be content to read so many only as he can read thoroughly, and to leave the rest untouched. Which should be read and which neglected, must be determined in each case by the abilities and attainments of the student.[36]

The timetable is tight but hardly impossible to complete. On average, the student would be expected to read for a separate subject in each term. None of the book lists is as long as those prepared at Oxford, but it is undoubtedly the case that the student would have had little time to dwell upon any one subject before moving to the next. There was hardly time for deep study.

While Hammond implied that the student would spend the greater part of his working time alone, and that he would have to chart the extent of his private reading for himself, the reality was probably less severe. Either through oral teaching or through the discussion of weekly essays the Regius Professor and the college teachers all offered their classes some personal supervision. Trinity College instituted an annual college examination in history, the administration of which from the late 1870s was shared with King's. They were accompanied in 1886 by St John's College, in what then became known officially as the Inter-collegiate Examination in History, run independently of the board. On payment of a small fee, members of any college were allowed to sit it, and all but a tiny handful of students did so. As a result of these developments almost every student's work was checked on a weekly or fortnightly basis, and, on a more general level, his progress would be evaluated at the close of each academic year.[37]

Timetable, reading matter and teaching established, what kind of knowledge was expected of the student? Deborah Wormell has suggested that the Cambridge examination papers in history demanded not so much precise knowledge of historical detail as a capacity for making informed judgements upon complex problems. As an overall impression this carries some weight. But a closer inspection prompts some reservations. There is a division between two types of question paper. It corresponds neatly with the division of subject matter between history and the cognate sciences. While the questions on the cognate sciences closely represent

Dr. Wormell's views, the history examination papers tell another, different story, one which was to lead to agitation for Tripos reform.[38]

The paper on English history was regarded as most important. To confer a knowledge of English history was deemed to be one of the Tripos's foremost functions. Yet the questions set for examination demanded little more than precise knowledge of detail. Two such examples taken from the paper set in December 1876 read:

1. Sketch the career of Godwine, and criticize his conduct.

12. Trace the course of Canning as a party politician.[39]

The paper's format changed little over ten years. Questions called for a detailed knowledge of the chief facts of particular reigns or epochs. This is not to say that the paper did not require from the student a great deal of work and effort. But it was 'an effort of memory' coupled with a facile power of expression.

The trend is evident in the other examination papers in history. All proliferate with questions beginning, 'Enumerate . . .', 'How did . . .', 'Give a short account of . . .'. Only the paper set by Seeley on 'The Foreign Possessions of England, 1756–83', demanded much above narrative detail. It mirrored much more closely the papers set for the cognate sciences.

The examination papers set on historical topics suggest that the study was pursued without any reference to the methods of historical investigation which both Ward and Stubbs had deemed so important in the process of mental training. Though knowledge of original sources might have been demonstrated in answers to such questions, the questions themselves were not designed to test it. The reasons are set out clearly by Hammond. He noted that the prescribed book list contained no reference to original sources – for the simple reason that they were too voluminous to mention.

The history teaching aimed simply at the production of leading facts and dates, something Seeley had denounced in his inaugural lecture. It could perhaps be explained by suggesting that the School was aiming to equip its students with a reasonably complete outline of English history, the necessary requirement of every well educated gentleman. But that was not the whole truth. The format of the

English history paper was less the product of design than the result of an unconscious lack of an alternative approach.

The end of the better intellectual training which Seeley and Hammond discussed was, as Dr Wormell has said, the formation of an informed opinion on large and interesting socio-political questions. This was to be gained primarily through the study of the cognate sciences, reinforced with a knowledge of general historical fact. The 'scientific' papers were not without their historical questions. But the history was used to illustrate principles of law or political practice, most of which had a direct bearing on contemporary legal, social and constitutional issues. Thus the constitutional history paper for 1879, in a question typical of most, asked the student to:

Mention the various means that have been adopted at various times to secure the frequent meeting of Parliament. How at the present day is this object effected?[40]

The organisation of other subjects was aligned to contemporary issues. The teacher of economic history was requested to keep his subject 'in the closest possible connection with the scientific principles of political economy'. The papers undoubtedly reflect this connection, but it was one which (in keeping with a growing number of economic historians) William Cunningham found increasingly difficult to maintain. The political philosophy, international law and the general essay papers reflect the all-pervading influence of Seeley and his teaching methods. They call predominantly for the definition of 'terms'. All presume, as Paul Fredericq noted, 'great cleverness on the part of the pupils'.[41]

Between 1873 and 1884, however, when the new complement of university lecturers were chosen, a reaction to this format set in. The Tripos had been an incubator. It had hatched historians. Some, like Thorneley, had come up through its ranks, and others, like Prothero, Cunningham, Gwatkin and to some extent Creighton and Maitland, learned their craft while teaching for it. They formed part of a new generation of writers. Not pioneers like Stubbs or Gardiner, but second-generation historians who learned, adopted and refined their methods, and who were now represented by the new *English Historical Review*. They had different ideas about the worth of a History

Tripos and the form it should assume.

Their first public spokesman was Mandell Creighton. He used the occasion of his inaugural lecture as Dixie Professor of Ecclesiastical History in January 1885 to state their position very clearly. His lecture was calculated to provoke argument. He ranged his own views about history against Seeley's public stance:

> In the study of history [he warned] . . . one caution is necessary. A study which has for its subject-matter the experience of the past must beware of seeking too direct results. The aim of all study is the education in method. It ought to develop the power of observation rather than supply opinions.

Creighton, like Seeley, maintained that it was less the subject matter of history than the method applied to it that was important in educational terms. Like Seeley, he thought that a thorough study of history could provide a firm basis for political opinion. But Creighton's idea of the nature of 'right judgement on the great issues of human affairs' was different. 'The study of history can give no mathematical certainty,' he said, 'but it can create a sober temper'. For Creighton, as for Stubbs, history developed the judgement. But judgement was not something which could be scientifically determined. It was a uniquely human quality which rested upon an intimate knowledge of man and his social environment. It was akin more to intuition than to a series of rules. It was a moral rather than a mathematical sense. While history could not be reduced to a series of formulae, a sympathetic and systematic reading of it could build the fund of knowledge and develop the qualities upon which right and balanced judgement was based. This capacity for judgement, said Creighton, was not the exclusive province of the politician, but was 'useful to many different classes of minds'.

Creighton did not stop there. Having criticised the aims and ends inherent in the Tripos, he criticised the methods of teaching. There were too many lectures, too many notebooks and too many manuals. Men must be taught to think, but not about the foundation of modern political thought. Creighton wanted to teach history and that through critical reflection on original sources. He hoped that 'a familiarity with the sources of history' would soon 'react upon the general course of reading prescribed for an examination'. This, he said, would put an end to 'cram', and better develop the cognitive processes. He issued a provocative challenge. 'The method by which this result is best to be attained,' he said, 'must depend upon the relations of that subject to the examinations of the university, and on the relation of the Professor to other teachers in the same subject.' Creighton had expressed his views. He had hinted that reform was the only course which could be taken to remedy basic deficiencies in the system. Who among the teaching staff would join him?[42]

The answer was not long coming. Just a week after his inaugural lecture the first in a lengthy series of articles appeared in the *Cambridge Review*. They predate the board's discussion of reform by almost a month, and are important for a number of reasons. The arguments outline the principles upon which reform and opposition to it were based. Creighton's lecture had been veiled in general terms. Names went unmentioned. Practical measures of reform remained undiscussed. Now the debate began. Accusations were levelled and failings assigned. The articles outline clearly the educational issues at stake, and go some way towards equating ideas about the nature and direction of reform to the practical details which comprised it. Their intended function was, as Prothero noted, to achieve 'a clear idea of the principles upon which a Tripos should be formed.'

These Prothero outlined. The key to deciding the nature of a study, he said, was to define its underlying aims, to fix the limits of the subject and then to demand a certain level of proficiency in it. The ensuing controversy hinged on the first two points. Neither Prothero nor the Tripos's other detractors would have denied that a history course should or could be of practical benefit to the student's later career. But most believed this to be a secondary, and in Prothero's case, an incidental benefit. To him the Tripos 'should keep a scientific and not a practical end primarily in view'. When he said that the Tripos should remain 'strictly scientific' Prothero meant that it ought to train the student in historical method, which cultivated thoroughness and powers of reasoning. We have, he insisted, 'paid too little attention to the methods of scientific discovery, and too much to the mere acquisition of knowledge'. Used in this way, the term 'science' was an updated restatement of the ideals of a liberal education, which had advocated rigour and thoroughness, and had signified a belief in methodical study as the best means towards achieving a sound 'mental training'.

Critics believed that the nature of the Tripos implied 'the pursuit of a practical aim at the expense of scientific perfection', and that the limits of the study were defined in relation to that aim. While most were prepared to concede 'that History pure and simple will not supply a satisfactory mental training', they felt that the cognate sciences were too numerous, and dominated to such an extent that history, which could be a valuable means towards the end of mental training, was virtually ignored. Prothero was adamant: 'the methods of historical research, the valuation and comparison of authorities, and the sifting of evidence' were the 'processes by which History vindicates its claim to be a science, and which confer educational value on an historical training'. At Cambridge these processes were ignored. A First Class Honours degree in history could be obtained without knowledge of original authorities. Prothero and other critics thought this scandalous. But their invective rested upon shifting ground. They maintained that historical techniques were an important means of training the mind and its faculties, but then went further. The Historical Tripos ought to qualify the student 'as a teacher of the subject, or as a further investigator of some branch of the same'. The Tripos should be a training ground for historical teachers and historians.

These aims underlay the specific proposals for reform. The history teacher needed a well stocked body of historical fact. He must appreciate the continuity of history. A general knowledge of European history was essential. It ought to convey the 'mainstream of historical development, the general characteristics of each age and nation and their relations with each other, the place which each holds in universal history'. The historian must learn historical method. Therefore the detailed study of a selected period, read with reference to the original authorities, was essential. These improvements could be implemented only if the number of cognate sciences designated for study was reduced.[43]

In response Seeley changed his method of approach. He did not attempt to defend what he had helped to establish. He stated very simply that in order to build a platform for historical study at

Cambridge it had been necessary to create a Tripos in some shape or form. Indeed, he said, the current debate proved not that the administrators had failed but, on the contrary, that they had succeeded. Prothero expressed himself baffled by the logic of Seeley's remark, and thought it a rather mystical and prophetic attempt to dodge the issue, but he was wide of the truth. Seeley was not referring to the success of the Tripos in training men to a particular ideal, but rather to the fact that agitated discussion about it proved that as a medium of education it was well enough established for persons to consider it worth worrying about.

Seeley can, however, be charged with a certain degree of elusiveness. He expressed the view that the Tripos was simply a game, a series of hoops through which, in the pursuit of larger aims, students and teachers must jump. Students wanted degrees, teachers wanted to confer some educational benefit. Seeley said that his own ideas about the purpose and value of an historical education did not require a Tripos. Indeed, he professed himself unconcerned with it. It was something which could have impaired the effectiveness of his own teaching, though conveniently it had not done so.

Seeley did not deny the reformers the validity of their criticisms. He was aware that opposition to the Tripos was strong, and that some changes would occur. His defence of the system was by implication only. He maintained his own belief that original sources were an important part of an historical education. But examinations were the crux of every Tripos. How, without a heavy reliance on memory, could a knowledge of historical technique be tested in examinations? It was a telling point. Was not the memorising of passages from original sources the same sort of activity as learning them from books? A dissertation would most certainly prove the extent of a candidate's mastery of research techniques, but, said Seeley:

> If we succeeded in laying proper stress on original documents we should meet the needs of the small advanced class, but in my opinion, we should sacrifice the larger number, who have usually not reached, and perhaps never will reach, that stage of historical study.

In this Seeley found support.[44] He further criticised the idea of teaching 'universal history'. It could only degenerate into a study of facts and how to cram them. Seeley was adamant. If teachers had definite ends in sight, then they could, within the general confines of the Tripos, 'do their own thing'. 'If the results we obtain at present are not altogether satisfactory,' he said:

> and this seems to me almost a matter of course, when I consider the newness of the subject, the want of text books, and the short time allowed for preparation – I should advise that we should study to get the ablest lecturers, that these lecturers should lecture as well as possible, that they should produce more original work, and for this purpose should not allow themselves to be hampered by the Tripos. . . . In short, I think the school wants more vitality, not more artificial machinery.[45]

Seeley was suggesting tacitly that original sources could be introduced by lecturers in their own time and in their own way. Creighton was doing it, and Seeley made similar efforts in his conversation class. He was making a subtle plea for moderation. He was suggesting that reform need not be made such a dramatic issue. He ended his article with a plea for unity. Whatever the outcome of the discussion, the future of historical teaching in Cambridge depended upon a united teaching body. Without it the labours of the last ten years were wasted.

Nevertheless Gwatkin, Prothero, Creighton and Browning had all proved that even if the Tripos were ignored it would not go away. As Prothero noted, 'It is the business of college lecturers to prepare candidates for examinations, and they must teach accordingly.' Gwatkin, like Creighton, suggested that 'examinations can be made a good guide for all the work which undergraduates are old enough to do'. If more stress was to be placed on the methods of historical research, then those methods must be tested by examination. Reform of the Tripos, he said, would provide 'a hopeful means of raising the study of history from its present low estate in Cambridge'. Practical measures to this end were not long in coming.[46]

On 24 February 1885 Prothero called for a special meeting of the board to discuss changes in the Tripos. It was convened on 2 May. Four vital principles of reform were discussed and agreed upon. First, the present examination system was adjudged unsatisfactory because 'insufficient attention . . . [was] paid to the study of original authorities', thereby ignoring the fundamental basis upon which the subject rested. The second reflected a compromise. While it was agreed that the study of original authorities would become a more prominent feature of the Tripos, it was concluded also that political philosophy would be retained as a 'non-alternative' subject. If the historians were to have a larger share of the Tripos those in favour of teaching politics would ensure that their own study was not neglected. The third major principle upon which the board agreed was that there should be a reduction in the number of subjects prescribed for examination. They concurred in the belief that the strain the present Tripos imposed upon the student's memory was excessive, and that the multiplicity of subjects encouraged 'a tendency to superficiality'. The means by which this reduction would be accomplished, without damaging the efficiency of the Tripos as a thorough and exacting test, was embodied in the fourth principle. It would be worked through a system of alternative subjects. Each faction would lay claim to certain 'essential' papers, and the middle ground would be left open to the student's own predilection. He would be allowed to choose between theoretical and historical topics. This was a face-saving compromise. Neither party would have a controlling share in the subjects of the Tripos, but neither party was being asked to stand down. History was now recognised as a rigorous pursuit separated from other subjects by its own distinct techniques, while it continued to be the focus of other historically based, cognate sciences which as yet lacked their own Tripos. Honour was even, and the teaching staff seemingly united in the common goal of keeping the Tripos running.[47]

The final result was that the candidate for Honours would sit two papers on the constitutional history of England. The old outline paper of English political history was discarded as 'superficial', and the constitutional law and history paper was expanded to cover two papers, with a division at the reign of Henry VII. Now a more detailed knowledge of English history could be demanded of candidates. As at Oxford, question papers were designed to test a knowledge of the sources for English history. Though some questions continued to refer past history to present points of law, they were reduced significantly.

Following pressure from Cunningham, and against a strong background of dissent in the historical world at large, economic history was separated from political economy, which, with the 'General Theory of Law and Government and the Principles of International Law', became an alternative subject. Economic history was divorced from its direct connection with economic science. Cunningham had won the first of many battles against Marshall in what was to be a long campaign.

In deference to Seeley the compulsory paper in political science went unopposed. All students must sit an examination 'composed of questions bearing on the inductive study of political institutions'. But there the compulsory study of the cognate sciences ceased.

All students were required to read for one special subject, in which 'one or more original authorities will be specified, one of which will, if possible, be in a foreign language'. They were then faced with a choice. Those who were interested in history could opt to read for a second 'special'; those who were not would study the two alternative cognate sciences.

Even the two essay papers reflected the compromise. One comprised very general political/philosophical questions. It reflected the idea that the student should learn to form ideas on large considerations of practical importance. The second dealt with the subjects of English history which were left uncovered by the constitutional papers.

The 'historians' had their original sources, the 'politicians' retained a measure of theory. But the agreement was hardly far-sighted. Much to Prothero's dismay, there was still no course on European history; still the candidate was burdened heavily with examinations. Most believed further modifications would undoubtedly follow.

Whatever the strength of lingering discontents, important educational principles had been established. A university History Tripos should act as an intellectual map. It should mark clearly the contours of historical science, and students should be required to follow them closely. History was now recognised clearly to be a developing, research-based discipline, and it was agreed that students should be aware of the distinctive processes as well as the distinctive products of historical research. Both had a positive educational value. It was accepted, though by no means unanimously, that a university history school ought to equip a good student to do further independent historical work; to extend and refine the map of historical knowledge. But one question remained. What form ought that training to take? How would the balance between the aims and ideals of a general liberal education and the increasingly technical demands of a research training be struck?

NOTES TO CHAPTER 5

1   C.U.L.U.A., U.P. 40, fol. 80, fol. 344.

2   C.U.L.U.A., U.P. 41, fol. 134.

3   C.U.L. U.A., Guard Book (History), C.U.R. 28.10 (1).

4   C.U.L. U.A., U.P. 41, fol. 134.

5   F. W. Maitland, 'Why the history of English law is not written', in The Collected Papers of F. W. Maitland, vol. I, ed. H. A. L. Fisher (Cambridge, 1911), pp. 480–510.

6   E. C. Clark, Public Orator, C.U. Reporter, 1 May 1872, p. 269.

7   Seeley's lecture 'The teaching of politics' was published in Macmillan's Magazine, XXI, November 1869–April 1870, pp. 433–44, and subsequently reprinted in J. R. Seeley, Lectures and Essays (London, 1870), pp. 290–317 (291). References are to the latter.

8   H. Sidgwick, 'The theory of a classical education', and J. R. Seeley, 'Liberal education in universities', in Essays on a Liberal Education, ed. F. W. Farrar (London, 1867), pp. 81–144, 145–78. C.U.L. U.P. 41, 21 November 1867. Arts School debate, E. C. Clark: 'the tone of the book showed that the University was not quite en rapport with the thoughts of the younger generation'.

9   Seeley, Lectures and Essays, pp. 293–4.

10   Seeley, Lectures and Essays, p. 295.

11   Seeley, Lectures and Essays, p. 296.

12   W. Stubbs, Seventeen Lectures on Medieval and Modern History third edition (Oxford, 1900), p. 9, p. 82, p. 122.

13   T. H. Huxley, 'A liberal education and where to find it', in Collected Essays by T. H. Huxley, vol. III (London, 1893), pp. 76–110 (109). Herbert Spencer, Herbert Spencer on Education, ed. F. A. Cavenagh (Cambridge, 1932), p. 15, p. 40. For Seeley in 1863 see; J. R. Seeley, Classical Studies as an Introduction to the moral Sciences (London, 1864).

14   Seeley, Lectues and Essays, pp. 302–5 (302).

15   Peter Slee, History as a Discipline, pp. 312–21.

16   W. E. Heitland, After many Years: a Tale of Experience gathered in the course of an obscure Life (Cambridge, 1926), p. 137.

17   Reporter, 43, 1 May 1872, pp. 268–9, C.U.L. U.A., 28.10, fol. 2 (9).

18   A. W. Ward, 'The study of History at Cambridge', in The Collected Papers of Sir A. W. Ward [in five volumes] (Cambridge, 1921, v. pp. 244–256. (p. 251).

19   C.U.L. U.A., C.U.R. 28.10, fol. 2 (a), Reporter, 1 May 1872, p. 268.

20   Reporter, 1 May 1872, p. 268.

21   A. W. Ward, Suggestions towards the Establishment of a History Tripos (Cambridge, 1872), pp. 14–15. Collected Papers, V, p. 253.

22   Reporter, 65, 18 December 1872, pp. 131–6 (p. 132).

23   J. O. McClachlan, 'The Cambridge Historical Tripos', Cambridge Historical Journal, IX, No. 1, 1947, pp. 78–99 (p. 84).

24   C.U.L. U.A., C.U.R. 28.10, fol. 3 (1) A. W. Ward On the Proposed Historical Tripos, 1 February 1873.

25   Reporter, 6, 11 February 1873, pp. 88–9. B. E. Hammond, 'The Historical Tripos', in The Student's Guide to the University of Cambridge, third edition (Cambridge, 1874), pp. 421–38 (p. 423).

26   *Reporter*, 7, 18 February 1873, pp. 95–9 (p. 97).

27   Royal Historical Society, London, Papers of G. W. Prothero, pp. 1 / 2 / Henry Jackson to G. W. Prothero, 5 February 1873.

28   King's College, Cambridge, Archives, Educ. Cncl. Mins. 1861–78, Min. 20 January, 1875 (p. 81), 25 February 1875 (p. 82), 12 February 1876 (p. 92), 6 March 1876 (p. 92).

29   R.H.S. pp./2/1, Seeley to Prothero, undated. For B. Walker see S. J. C. Concl. Book, 1846–72, 2 February 1869. For I.C.L. pilot scheme see K.C.C. E.C. Mins., 1861–78, p. 30; for formal university wide extension in 1875 see S.J.C. D104, 109–17, fol. 116–17.

30   R.HS. pp /2/1, Seeley to Prothero, undated.

31   K.C.C. E.C. Min., 1861–78, Min. 11 March 1875 (p. 84), 16 October 1875 (p. 88). Report, 25 November 1875, Min 6 March 1876 (p. 92).

32   K.C.C. E.C. Min., 1861–78, Report 15 May 1877. Seeley Library, Cambridge, Minutes of the Special Board for History and Archaeology, November 1876–May 1893, Min. 30 November 1876. For the O.B. see Ian Anstruther, *Oscar Browning: a biography* (London 1983).

33   Seeley Library, Minutes, 1876–93, 24 November 1879. Report, 5 February 1880, Min. 30 January 1883, Min. 13 February 1883.

34   Seeley Library, Minutes, 26 November 1883, 8 May 1884.

35   Hammond, 'The Historical Tripos', pp 428–36.

36   Hammond, 'The Historical Tripos', pp. 432–3, (p. 433).

37   K.C.C. E.C. Min., 1879–82, 24 May 1879 (p. 21), 30 April 1881 (p. 109). *Return to the House of Commons relating to the Universities of Oxford and Cambridge* 1886, Part B, pp. 47–8, S.J.C. D.100, 77 (1893). Trinity College, Cambridge 30361–.

38   Deborah Wormell, *Sir John Seeley and the Uses of History* (Cambridge, 1979), p. 113–14.

39   *Cambridge University Examination Papers* 1876–7, vol. VI, p. 135.

40   C.U. E.P., 1879–80, vol. IX, p. 115, q. 6.

41   *Cambridge University (Report of Syndicate) returned to the House of Commons* 12 June 1876, p. 29. Paul Fredericq, *The Study of History in England and Scotland*, Johns Hopkins University Studies in Historical and Political Science, Fifth Series, X, (Baltimore, 1887), p. 24.

42   Mandell Creighton, 'The teaching of ecclesiastical history', in *Historical Lectures and Addresses* (London, 1903), pp. 2–28 (p. 16, p. 21, pp. 23–4).

43   G. W. Prothero, 'The Historical Tripos', *Cambridge Review*, VI, No. 139, 28 January 1885, pp. 163–6.

44   J. R. Seeley, 'The Historical Tripos', C.R. VI, 141, 11 February 1885, pp. 194–5. See also C.R., VI, 141, pp. 200–1.

45   Seeley, C.R., VI, 141, p. 194.

46   G. W. Prothero, 'The Historical Tripos: a reply', C.R., VI, 142, 18 February 1885, pp. 211–14. H. M. Gwatkin, 'The Historical Tripos', C.R., VI, 141, 11 February 1885, pp. 199–200.

47   Seeley Library, Minutes, 2 May 1885.

CHAPTER 6

'A class examination of high character'
THE OXFORD SCHOOL OF MODERN HISTORY, 1867–95

Between 1869 and 1885 the Oxford History School was transformed completely. When history separated finally from law it became the sole basis of a new restructured examination School in which its own subject matter and distinctive methodological techniques replaced the close reading and commentary upon set texts. From its lowly position as a modern adjunct of the traditional School of Literae Humaniores – a curious, interesting and 'easy school for rich men' – modern history became an independent and rigorous academic discipline.

Many have accredited this transformation to Professor Stubbs.[1] But the credit is not his. Stubbs's effect on the method and system of Oxford history teaching was marginal and at most indirect. The basis of the restructured School was laid in the seven years before Stubbs's appointment to the Regius Chair, when three distinct movements gained momentum.

The first was a methodological shift in the teaching of history, away from an exclusive reliance on texts to the study of periods and subjects. It was advocated in public by Burrows in 1862, five years before Stubbs's appointment as Regius Professor. Burrows had made it clear, however, that under the present administrative arrangements which bound history to law no such change could successfully be effected. As it stood in 1862 history could be developed no further. Similar frustrations were expressed by teachers of law. Since 1854 they had complained of an imbalanced allocation of teaching time that restricted legal studies to an elementary study of outdated texts.[2] Like history, legal studies were developing rapidly, so much so that Montagu Bernard, Chichele Professor of International Law, claimed they should have their 'proper place' in Oxford as 'a distinct science.'[3]

The second, then, was a practical movement for separation. Begun in the early '50s it gained its most significant boost from the statutory legislation of 1864. The examination statute was promulgated mainly to release students of classics from a less weighty but time-consuming and expensive second study. While the legislation afforded the newer schools an opportunity to reconsider their structure and format, no guidelines for expansion were proposed. It was clear, however, that while history was coupled with law little fundamental change was possible. Both disciplines were too wide-ranging in subject matter, too disparate in method, too distinct in technique to be treated in a thorough and systematic manner. Though under the new regulations students were required to pass Moderations within ten rather than twelve terms, any extra time they might have had at their disposal for deeper study was taken up with reading for an extra special historical subject and a more detailed treatment of Smith's political economy. While its status was elevated, the substance of the School remained substantially unchanged. Students simply studied more of the same, and this exaggerated the old disputes. The development of sound historical teaching was being held back by an outdated coupling of two subjects approaching academic maturity. Law appeared after 1864 to have declined rather than risen in importance. To continue to limit the bulk of instruction to Blackstone and Justinian was an anachronism. A strong lobby insisted that the teaching of law at university ought to be based on general principles rather than rote learning of boundless detail. As E. A. Freeman put it, 'an examination in "Law and Modern History" is about as much an harmonious whole as would be an examination in Law and Hydrostatics, or in Phebotomy and Modern History'.[4]

The problem was considered officially in 1868, when the Hebdomadal Council appointed a committee to consider the general subject of university examinations. It reported in 1870 and recommended that for the mutual encouragement of both disciplines they should be cultivated separately. The proviso was that:

> The examination in the Section or School of History, shall always include some portion of Modern History carefully studied with reference to the original authorities, the General History of Europe during some period or periods, the Constitutional History of England, Political Economy, and passages of translation from French or German historical writers.[5]

There was no mention of books.

The third important movement was the gradual emergence of a body of specialist history teachers, every one developing his own specialism within the confines of the broader syllabus. This too was an accidental by-product of the examination statute.

After 1864 students who read for the final School of Law and Modern History did so not only to complete the formal requirements for a degree but also to secure their final Class. The School took on a new importance, and both students and their colleges regarded it more seriously. The teachers' work load increased considerably. More students read more methodically, and even experienced tutors found the pressures excessive. Thomas Fowler explained that:

> the school of law and modern history . . . requires a competent teacher in law, a competent teacher in political economy, a competent teacher in modern history; at least one; and I question whether one man could undertake the whole range of modern history, and whether you ought not to have two instructors in modern history, one for each period.[6]

This colleges could hardly contemplate. Some had elected one tutor or lecturer; to appoint more was financially unthinkable. The result, complained W. L. Newman, was that 'college lecturers have to deal with a very wide field . . . I feel perpetually that I am dealing with subjects with which I have no claim to deal at all.' The diverse combination of books and special subjects clearly made it difficult for a college tutor to offer every student in his charge detailed instruction in all the available subjects. The solution said Newman was not to increase the number of tutors in each college but rather to combine existing resources and to specialise.[7]

Combination of colleges for the purpose of shared teaching was by no means unheard-of. Newman taught students from New College in 1866. The Warden and Tutors' Committee of New College were concerned that students of history should receive some instruction but were not yet quite convinced that numbers were sufficient to warrant the appointment of their own lecturer.[8] What was new in the ensuing scheme, however, was the idea of specialisation. Every lecturer who joined the voluntary association of college teachers agreed to open his lectures free of charge to his colleagues' students. Lecturers were then able to divide the subjects of study between them and to concentrate in greater detail on their own appointed specialism.

The scheme began in a small way. Contrary to received opinion, it was not initiated or even encouraged by Stubbs.[9] Robert Laing of Corpus Christi told the university commissioners that it 'originated in my rooms. Mr Talbot, now the warden of Keble, and Mr. Shadwell of Oriel, and Mr. Creighton, who was at Merton, and myself, I think, set it going, and we set it going as an experiment.'[10]

The experiment was a success, and it soon attracted the support of other colleges all alive to its practical and financial benefits. New College gave H. B. George formal permission to join in 1869,[11] and by 1870 the list had expanded to include Sidney Owen and G. W. Kitchen of Christ Church, Charles Boase of Exeter and the two professors Stubbs and Burrows. Boase and Shadwell covered English history, with some help from Stubbs and Burrows. George and Owen took on the law teaching, and Burrows, Talbot, Kitchen, George, Laing and Creighton all offered instruction in one of the special subjects.[12] But the scheme was not inspired by the Regius Professor, rather by the pressures of a restructured curriculum. Neither Stubbs nor Burrows joined it until the second year of operation, by which time the tone of Oxford history teaching had been set. From its lowly beginnings in 1868 the Modern History Association rose to dominate the practical running and administration of the new School.

The revised Oxford syllabus was divided into 'three heads of examination', what Stubbs called:

a continuous reading of our national History, second an epochal treatment of a portion of general European History, and thirdly, the special study of some character or period in the original authorities.[13]

Each 'head' was based on a particular conception of the term 'history' and was intended to dispel doubts about whether the subject 'by itself was substantive enough to furnish the training for a class examination of high character'[14] by conferring a particular type of educational benefit.

In educational terms the key concept was the Arnoldian view of modern history as continuous contiguous national development. Modern history was held to begin with the fall of Rome. The collapse of the empire was a curtain separating past and present; it put an end for ever to the possibility of one world State. Small autonomous nations appeared as the moving force in European history, which from the fall of Rome became the continuous process of multilateral, multinational development. Stubbs maintained that 'in this new and modern living world there has been since the era began, such a continuity of life and development that hardly one point in its earliest life can be touched without the awakening some chord in the present'. The idea of the continuity of national history – of history as process – conferred dignity and substance to what it was felt might otherwise be regarded as a random series of facts and dates.[15] Nevertheless the idea of history as a body of important information and even as a meaningful continuous process was not a sufficient base upon which to rest the discipline. The study of history must also be thorough and demanding. It must encourage depth as much as breadth of study.

The solution was found by dividing the study of English history into two aspects; into political and constitutional papers. Constitutional history formed what W. J. Ashley called 'the backbone of the School'.[16] It offered a calibrated framework upon which to base the study of national history. The English constitution was the thread upon which national development was hung; it was the vehicle of continuity. While constitutional history involved studying the machinery of government, parliamentary institutions and national law, political history was defined almost by default as those aspects of national history not included under the former heading – the reigns of monarchs, the development of the Church and the growth of foreign policy.

The division of subject matter was intended primarily to express a division of educational function. When in 1883 Richard Lodge of Brasenose College moved that the distinction between political and constitutional history be abolished the division was defended by H. B. George, who reminded him that the constitutional paper involved the student in detailed knowledge of a difficult subject, something which was a stiff test of a student's ability to master a complex technical study, whereas political or general history tested his ability to deal with larger historical issues.[17] Constitutional history was taught and studied as a highly technical subject, which was designed to give 'a strength and dignity to the School which it might otherwise lack'. It introduced the student to a new and difficult language. 'The student when he plunges into it,' said W. J. Ashley:

> seems to enter a forest of *gesiths* and *gemots*, of *assizes* and *justiciars*, of *tenths* and *fifteenths*, where the paths all run into another, and lead nowither.[18]

In general the examination papers bear out these claims. Constitutional history involved for the most part direct questions on specific points of detail. For instance:

> Mention the chief codes promulgated in the Anglo-Saxon period. What circumstances called them forth, and on what conception of law do they rest?

> Draw out the exact effects of the Norman Conquest by comparing (1) the manor with the soken, (2) barons with thegns, (3) the Curia Regis with the Witenagemot.

> What new forms of taxation were introduced in the 15th and 16th centuries, and how far did they imply new principles?

> Show from Charles II's reign how the effective power of the crown was limited at the Restoration.

> Examine, from a constitutional point of view, Fox's conduct on the Regency bill and Pitt's plan of restrictions upon the power of the Regent.

Some questions involved Latin or French translation, and all required some knowledge of original sources, though these would be found in Stubbs's *Charters*. Most questions required specific answers, containing direct points of technical detail. There was little scope for conjecture, even when questions appeared to be more general:

> Was the principle that the king should 'live of his own' favourable or not to constitutional progress?
>
> Illustrate from the history of the East India Company the growth of the power of the House of Commons.

They still demanded knowledge of a specific aspect of constitutional history, and enquired as to its role in the process of national development.[19]

The question papers on political history, however, were of a more general nature. For the most part they expected a different type of answer, and offered a different perspective of national history:

> Trace the foreign relations of England from the reign of Alfred to that of Ethelred II inclusive, and explain the motives of the kings.
>
> What was the nature of English chivalry and its effect upon society at different periods?
>
> Trace the relations of England with Holland from the reign of James I to that of William III.
>
> Trace the stages through which the movement for the abolition of slavery passed.[20]

The epochal treatment of European history followed a similar pattern. Students studied a short period of 'foreign history', investigated the interplay of European nations, and analysed the character and varied development of different States. Study was concentrated on the nation State, and on the actions of great men as agents of political destiny. Examination papers reveal a mixture of 'specific' and 'general' questions – some relating to long-term developments and others to a short series of particular actions or events, these last illustrating a second view of history as a series of specific actions taking place in a particular location at a particular time.

The third part of the syllabus dealt with another aspect of the term 'history'. In this case it was 'history' as the process of discovery. The special subject was drawn up in recognition of the fact that the 'professional' study of history involved a definite method, and that that method rested upon the study and criticism of original sources.

G. W. Kitchin of Christ Church put it succinctly. 'The object of a special subject in the History School is to compel young men to read the original authorities.' The special subject was by no means the most important, or even the most substantial, element of the course. To Stubbs it was no more than an introduction, albeit a valuable one, to historical study. Its inclusion in the syllabus was a recognition that if history had not yet attained 'the dignity of a science', then there was at least 'an art of writing History and an art of reading it; and the educational use of it is an exemplification of the art'.[21]

The only significant changes made to the syllabus between 1872 and 1895 came in 1885. They did not change the character of the School. The period of 'General European History' was shortened and was to be read alongside a corresponding and similarly abridged period of English history. The change was made, said A. L. Smith, in order to ensure that the student grasped the close relationship between developments in English and European history.[22]

Since 1872 candidates had been requested to read political economy, and in 1885 this was combined with political science in a single paper. It was believed that the two subjects were complementary, and if read together would offer the student 'a mental tonic', similar to that provided by logic in the School of Literae Humaniores. It was said that political science involved a form of mental exercise which could not be secured by the exclusive study of pure history. It involved abstract reasoning from first principles. At Oxford the study rested on a few set texts and unlike Cambridge was not studied 'inductively', that is to say, with reference to the historical process.[23]

The restructured syllabus had far-reaching effects for the growing body of history lecturers. Once commentary on set texts no longer formed the basis of the teaching for the School the catechetical lecture became an outmoded form of discourse. The history teacher's new function was to convey information and to provide the outline of a particular subject. Robert Laing noted that though lecturers might still criticise statements and arguments conveyed in books, after the change of syllabus men were expected to tackle the bulk of the literature themselves. Lectures were intended as an introduction to the period or subject under consideration, and were to 'supplement and control the study of the great standard historians of English and continental affairs'.[24]

The new system brought with it increased demands on the lecturer. Subjects were broader and more numerous. They had to be taught in greater detail, and consequently required deeper preparation and more reading.[25] These factors enhanced the value of the Modern History Association. It was ideally suited to the demands of the new syllabus. Whereas under the catechetical system the lecturer could teach only as quickly as the slowest could learn, under the new system the teacher could administer as easily to the needs of fifty as to the needs of five. As colleges responded to history's new-found status by creating lecturers in the subject, so these lecturers joined the Modern History Association. Within two years of the first final examination in the new School membership had risen to thirteen. On joining the scheme Tutors were asked to submit their proposed course of lectures to the voluntary secretary of the association. Though no formal division of the subject was imposed upon them, the younger men were expected to lecure on the gaps. In 1874 every aspect of the new syllabus was covered by lectures of some sort. By 1879 only two colleges of eighteen in Oxford were without a history lecturer, and specialisation had become still more refined.[26]

The student would be advised by his college tutor as to the lectures he should attend. A register of attendance was kept. Failure to attend meant an unpleasant taste of college discipline.[27] While the combined lecture scheme created a wider audience for the college teacher, he was still required to supervise the progress of students from his own college. C. W. Boase of Exeter College explained that 'Each history teacher receives essays, and answers to questions from his own men, but not from men of other colleges.' Though H. B. George blamed a generation of bashful men for its demise, at Oxford at least, personal supervision of a whole lecture class was not possible, nor was it considered desirable. Though they acted in concert the history teachers remained college men. Their loyalty and responsibility were to their college. The weekly essay system provided a close contact between tutor and pupil, and helped to maintain a traditionally strong college bond.[28]

The combined lecture scheme had two particularly important effects on the administration of the Oxford School. It raised once

more the important and particularly sensitive issue of the relationship between tutor and professor in departmental organisation.
And it brought into question the relationship between the collegiate
and faculty structure.

Since the foundation of the Law and Modern History School
teaching had been the sole province of the college tutor. Through
their unwillingness to adopt the catechetical method Vaughan and
Goldwin Smith had displayed a marked indifference to the needs of
the student reading for the Schools. The organisation of inter-college
teaching was the result of tutorial effort and industry. Through it the
tutors gained an effective hold of the discpline. It was one which
they did not intend to relinquish.

Nevertheless, in 1872 Boards of Studies were created. They were
founded in recognition of the fact that managing the developing
studies required a measure of expertise. Different studies were
recognised as having different methods, and their regulation as
requiring specialist advice. But in 1872 through the board structure
the professorial body emerged as leaders of their respective disciplines. The History Board comprised the Regius Professor of
Modern History, both Chichele Professors, the Professors of Ecclesiastical History, Political Economy and Anglo-Saxon, three examiners
and three co-opted members. The tutors might have four or five
representatives on the board, but the balance of power lay with the
professorial body. The Regius Professor was the board's ex-officio
head. He held the casting vote. From a position of splendid isolation
the professors had emerged as potentially the controlling factor in
the development of university studies.[29]

The powers of the Boards of Studies were limited to prescribing
books, periods and special subjects. They could do little to control
the machinery of teaching, which was the province of the Modern
History Association. Nevertheless, with the demise of the catechetical lecture both professor and tutor shared the same basic function –
to convey information. The tutors saw this as a possible threat to
their own position; the first step to departmental and therefore
professorial organisation of lecture lists. After 1872 the association
closed ranks in an effort to nullify the influence of the professor on
what they regarded as their own exclusive function.

The tensions between tutor and professor were evidently strong.

Burrows wanted to teach. He felt that as professor he could offer students 'higher teaching'. He wished to compare 'periods of history with one another', and to deal with subjects in 'a comprehensive way'. But very quickly he came to believe that the system was against him. The tutors administered a system of mutual self-help. They relayed men between their own classes. While he did not suggest that men were physically prevented from attending professorial lectures, he knew that attendance was neither compelled nor suggested. Stubbs told a similar story. 'I have to join in the professorial chorus of complaint ...' he said. 'The professorial and tutorial systems have not yet dovetailed into one another with all the completeness that could be wished.' He had:

> sometimes felt a little hurt that, after preparing and advertising a good course of lectures ... I have had to deliver them to two or three listless men; sometimes I have felt hurt that, in the combined lecture list, when it appeared, I found the junior assistant tutor advertising a course on the same subject, or at the very same hours as my own.[30]

The tutorial side of the question is revealed in the evidence of the Royal Commission, gathered in 1877. The commission was concerned primarily with the better organisation of university teaching and the increased efficiency of departmental administration. The commission was toying with the idea that the best method by which both aims could be secured was through the extension and endowment of Chairs – a further threat to the autonomy and influence of the college teacher. The fears of the tutorial body are expressed clearly in the evidence of J. F. Bright.

Bright noted that, while the professors were asked to join the Educational Council which drew up the lecture lists at the close of each term, they 'practically have very little to do with the arrangement'. This is a euphemism. Translated, it means that a discipline can be organised without professors. He further maintained that the professors were originally 'intended to lead the organisation', and that 'we tried for several years to make a tolerably good arrangement, but it fell through'. This is manifestly untrue. Both Stubbs and Burrows were perfectly willing to lecture as part of the system, which, as we have seen, did not prove conducive to them. Bright then questioned the value and the status of the professor. What was his role? What authority was invested in him? Bright was clear on this. The history professors were just two more lecturers. They were simply 'individual members of our society; they have no authorised position enabling them to organise a scheme. They have no power nor have they any sort of position amongst us, beyond their personal position.' Here was a thinly disguised warning. The professor was but one man. His lecturing capability was no greater than that of any college tutor, of which there were many. The college tutors ran an efficient system, to which the professors had readily submitted. Their scheme was the continuation of a long tradition. College tutors had always taught undergraduates. They had expertise. It was their function. Bright was blunt. 'We do not like being turned from our natural course.' He feared that the commission would incorporate the inter-college system, currently an informal and purely voluntary agreement, into the formal structure of the university and in so doing would appoint a professorial head to run it. Bright warned that 'without a very strong professor of an organising turn of mind' the present system was not 'likely to assume a more definite form'. And he hinted darkly that:

> I do not think that a certain number of us would like to be disciplined . . . there are certain amongst us who would rather carry on their lectures upon their own ground than be brought into discipline by any professor whatever.[31]

Neither Stubbs nor Burrows was the 'strong professor of an organising turn of mind' which Bright feared. Both acquiesced in the fact that 'the men are principally taught by the college tutors'. Resistance was passive. Freeman, on the other hand, was exactly the type of professor that Bright and the others feared. But he arrived just too late to influence dramatically the relationship between professor and tutor, college and faculty.[32] The commission had weighed the evidence carefully, and, rather than change the existing system, decided to confirm it. The combined lecture scheme remained the basis of faculty teaching.

In 1873 Burrows had made the point that unless the professors could control the inter-collegiate system by making it a formal part of the university structure, the creation of more Chairs would be of little practical benefit to students.[33] The evidence of the tutors in

1877 simply confirmed his belief. But to create a formal inter-collegiate system would require substantial changes. There was little
chance that college lecturers would be given formal university status.
Expense was prohibitive. There was also little chance that the college
lecturers would submit peacefully to a higher authority. This would
mean relinquishing a long-cherished autonomy and alter dramatically the relationship between college and university. Colleges
regulated the duties of their employees. The creation of professorial
jurisdiction over individual college tutors would override this. The
commissioners compromised. They altered the structure of the
boards of studies and made lecturers answerable to them.

In 1881 four boards of faculty were created, to which ex-officio
and elected members were appointed in equal proportions. In 1885
the Board of the Faculty of Arts was subdivided into three sections,
of which one was Modern History. The boards were granted power
to draw up termly lecture lists and were also empowered with the
right of self-regulation with which they could supervise the internal
organisation of their own subject.

The various disciplines now had a bureaucratic hold upon their
own development. But where within each faculty did the balance of
power lie? The Board of History had twenty-eight members, half
ex-officio and half elected. But five of the former group had no
connection with either the curriculum or the examinations. As a
result, said C. H. Firth:

> they have no motive for attending [meetings] and do not attend, but the
> presence of their names in the list necessitates the addition of an elected
> member for each of them. The result is that the college teachers forming
> the elective element of the Board can determine every question con-
> nected with the study of Modern History exactly as they please.[34]

The constitution of the rearranged board meant that the lecturer was
placed nominally under a central authority. But the Modern History
Association continued to meet and organise exactly as it had before.
True, it now had to submit the lecture list to the faculty board for
official approval. But, with a working majority on the board, that
approval was nominal. The board simply made official what the
association had established informally. The lecturer's loyalty
remained with his college and his commitment to the faculty board

simply confirmed it. Though the implications of his statement were harsh, there was some little truth in J. E. T. Rogers's accusation that the Modern History Association was 'a board within the Board'. The association undoubtedly made efforts to ensure that its members acted in concert, and to ensure that, as a class, the tutors maintained their control of undergraduate instruction.

How, then, did the Tutors envisage the professor's function? In this they were unanimous. The professor should enhance the School's reputation for learning. He should leave teaching to the tutors, and devote himself to research and to writing the books which as teachers they had not the leisure to compile. One tutor expressed quite candidly the belief that 'the professor of modern history would prefer not to deliver lectures at all' and 'that the study of modern history would probably gain, because he would have more time for writing his books, which command a wider audience than the lectures which he delivers'.[35]

Robert Laing went further. Stubbs's major works, he said, were 'distinctly done with a view to our school'. He implied that the school had influenced the nature and content of Stubbs's life's work, and that Stubbs's chief function as professor was to write with the needs of the discipline in mind. The point is important.[36] By expressing a division of function between the art of teaching and the prosecution of research the tutors were defining the nature of their calling. John Higham has defined a profession as:

> a body of individuals with a particular skill, who by co-operative action establish and maintain their own standards of achievement instead of obeying some external authority.[37]

If we accept this definition, then the Modern History Association was a professional organisation. But as a body they grouped together as skilled teachers of history rather than as writers of it. The distinction is important. Historians of the period have tended to discuss the growth of an historical profession in contemporary terms. Today the professional historian is generally employed by an academic institution and is expected to teach, carry out research and to publish. It has been assumed that the process of 'professionalisation' began with the fragmentation of knowledge and specialisation, and with the corresponding extinction of the man of letters, and the evolution of a class of university-based academics.[38] Felix Gilbert believes that the university-based historical profession – which he defines as men who both taught and wrote history – emerged with the opening of the archives throughout Europe. Continental university development was heavily dependent upon government finance. Governments now grown nationalistic had a vested interest in their own past. They dictated that the archives be opened. And they directed university professors to them. Before they could settle comfortably into their role as educators Continental academics were invested with the dual function of teaching and researching.

In England, however, conditions were different. Universities were autonomous bodies. Gilbert maintains that in historiographical terms an 'amateur' tradition was upheld. That is to say, those who wrote history rarely taught it. Most historians produced books in their leisure time. Gilbert equates the development of an historical profession with the production of books. The profession developed slowly in England, he says, because history was less 'scientific' and because it was valued more as an educative discipline than as a 'science'.[39] While these factors undoubtedly influenced the peculiar development of an historical profession in England, they did not, as Gilbert suggests, preclude it. There was an historical profession in English universities. And it existed long before historical teachers considered it their duty to carry out historical research. It emerged at Oxford in the 1860s, with the formation of the combined lecture scheme.

Teachers began to assume a sense of corporate identity in the 1840s. In 1854 they founded their own association as a means of representing their views and stating their position. As a body they resisted successfully the claims of the University Commission to alter the basis of university teaching, and those of the Hebdomadal Board to deny them recognition as a separate class within the university. Circumstances forced the tutors to elaborate on their function. They regarded themselves not simply as teachers or instructors but as the vehicle of a liberal education. It was they who inspired the student to work, and to master his subject. The teacher had a vital role to play in the educative process. He was a specialist with professional skills and duties.

The Tutors' Association was formed to protect the tutors' role of instructor. It was not in their interest to disturb college autonomy. So when colleges could cope no longer with the rigours of varied and specialised departments of knowledge, tutors formed the combined lecture scheme. Through combining resources colleges maintained their autonomy and tutors their role as teachers of undergraduates.

The Modern History Association was a body of college teachers who combined to improve and to regulate professional standards of teaching, and to maintain a hold on their discipline. They were teachers whose primary aim was to push their students through the public examinations. They combined resources in recognition of the fact that they could achieve that aim only by rationalising the teaching process.

The creation of history as an independent academic discipline and then the growth in Oxford of the Modern History Association, and of a similar but less formal body in Cambridge, underpinned the rise of a distinct historical profession in England. It was a teaching profession. The fellowship reforms of 1882 simply confirmed a long-standing process. They ensured that most teachers did not look elsewhere for the prospect of a more secure livelihood. Many history tutors began with very little historical knowledge. Most had no intention of writing any substantial historical work, or of undertaking historical research. Teaching became its own career and brought its own rewards. A. L. Smith, perhaps the greatest and the best loved Oxford history teacher, wrote to his mother on 27 April 1879, the date of his election to a lectureship in modern history at Balliol:

> I am new to the work and not able to do it all unaided; but it will improve as I get more competent . . . there is a great opening in the University for the teaching of Modern History, which I have plunged into heart and soul, from mingled motives of necessity, ambition and interest in it.[40]

Smith had taken a first in classics in 1872, and a second in history in 1873–74. He simply wanted to teach. Modern history gave him the opening.

Though the distinction between teachers and researchers was most prominent at Oxford it also existed at Cambridge, though there its effects were mitigated to some degree by the enforced professorial participation in teaching for the Moral Sciences Tripos. At Cambridge the Regius Professor had been expected to teach undergraduates. The shortage of teaching capital under the new Tripos merely confirmed that trend. Furthermore, at Cambridge, where the teaching body was small, a greater proportion of college lecturers became involved in writing and research. But even lecturers like Prothero and Gwatkin agreed with those in Oxford like Smith and Boase. Their first duty was to their classes. Their testimony simply underlines the fact that they regarded themselves in the first instance as professional teachers. When the idea of the university as a place of research grew, many teachers began to consider it their duty to undertake original investigation. But while colleges appointed them to teach it remained a secondary aspect of their job. It was this seemingly obligatory division of function which underlay much of the controversy which ensued at the end of the century, and which will be discussed in the final section of this book.[41]

The curriculum was established and its ends were defined, if not always agreed upon unanimously. A body of teachers was well drilled to lead students through the syllabus. But how did students approach their studies? How were they taught? How did the teaching relate to the examination structure? In other words, what was it like to be a history student at Oxford between 1872 and 1895?

Having passed Moderations the student would expect to complete the requirements of the BA degree within two years. The first problem for the man reading history was how to organise his time efficiently. He had to prepare for nine examination papers in six subjects. Preparation involved three distinct and well-defined tasks: lectures, which would employ the student for the greater part of the morning; reading, which would take up the dilligent student's after-noons; and essay-writing. The schedule was tight. The student would first seek out his tutor for advice. Whoever his tutor, the student would have received similar instructions.

Written by college lecturers, two papers outlining course requirements and the best methods of completing them survive. One, written for the edification of outsiders, is by W. J. Ashley; the other, written to frighten away those students who believed history to be an easy option, is by C. H. Firth. The advice is remarkably similar. Both men worked on the principle that lectures formed an important introduction to the student's reading and that he should read for a subject while attending lectures on it. The Modern History Association arranged its lecture timetable accordingly. It adopted the principle that English History was the foundation of the syllabus. It should be studied first. Most benefit would be gained from the special subject if it was read when the student was practised in the art of reading and criticising history books and writing essays.

Firth suggested that students should begin to prepare themselves for the constitutional history papers as soon as Moderations were completed. Though the summer vacation might have been well earned, it must also be well spent – reading Stubbs, Freeman and Green. For those few students who might find such pursuits wearing Firth suggested that a little light relief could be found in the historical plays of Shakespeare.

The first year would be spent on the constitutional and political history of England, with the introductory work for the general period of European history to be taken up in the summer term. Reading for constitutional history would revolve around Stubbs's *Select Charters* and *Constitutional History*, and the English constitution according to Hallam, May and Bagehot. For political history Freeman's *Norman Conquest*, Green's *Short History of the English People* and Ranke, Macaulay and Bright's respective histories of England were the core texts. While beginning with these works, a student commencing his studies in 1886 (when Firth wrote his paper) would find that he would have to pick up his outline of political history either from his constitutional history lectures, or from his own reading. He would begin his first term by attending the lectures of Richard Lodge at Brasenose on 'Constitutional history from the beginning to Stephen'. The course was intensive – four lectures a week – but was concluded in four weeks, when the story was taken up by C. R. L. Fletcher of Magdalen. He lectured on the same days – Monday, Wednesday, Friday and Saturday – and at the same time – 10.00 a.m. – and carried the subject from Henry II to Edward I.

Returning from his Christmas break, the student would continue his constitutional course by attending the lectures of D. J. Medley at Balliol. Medley lectured on the period Edward II – Richard III on Tuesdays, Thursdays and Saturdays at 10.00, while H. B. George of New College lectured on Tudors and Stuarts on Mondays, Wednesdays and Fridays at the same time. Students who had read ahead might prefer to attend the classes run by Boase and A. H. Johnson, which offered a detailed analysis of Stubbs's *Charters*. But they were run at the same hour as the narrative lectures, and the student would have required some advice from his tutor as to which to attend.

The third term in the student's first year would probably have been his heaviest. He would be completing his constitutional course by attending the lectures of A. H. Johnson on the period 1688–1815 while reading the latter volumes of Hallam and those of May and Bagehot. He would also be reading and taking notes for the latter half of the political paper. Then he would begin a daunting course of reading for the general period. Firth noted that the most popular epochs were 1414–1610 and 1715–1815. The reading list for the latter is particularly voluminous, suggesting a perusal of some thirty-four works. The student would have attended the introductory lecture course delivered by A. H. Hassall in the hope of cutting a pathway through this forest of literature.

There was no rest in the long vacation. That must be spent revising the previous year's work, which (warned Ashley) formed 'the backbone of the School'. As a break from revision, reading for political science and the general period ought to be undertaken.

In the following term, the first of his second year, the student would be expected to complete those two subjects and to revise them in his Christmas vacation. On Thursdays and Saturdays he would attend the lectures of J. A. R. Marriot of Worcester on English history in the eighteenth century, and on Thursdays and Fridays at 11.00 those of A. H. Johnson of All Souls on the corresponding period of European History. He would then attend the course on political science offered by D. G. Ritchie on Tuesdays and Thursdays at 10.00 and that of W. J. Ashley on political economy delivered on Mondays and Thursdays at 4.45 p.m.

The reading for political science and political economy, though by no means as bulky as that required for the core courses, involved a thorough knowledge of Aristotle's *Politics*, Hobbes's *Leviathan*, Bluntschli's *Origin of the Modern State*, Maine's *Ancient Law*, and Mill's *Political Economy*. Ashley noted that while Mill remained the chief source for political economy, the concept of rules of economic development which were true throughout all ages was being revised by economic historians. He advised all students to read the treatises of Cunningham, Rogers and Toynbee in order that they understand this development. Clearly, much reading had to be completed in the vacations.

The special subject, which was intended to lead students to the original authorities, and which Firth suggested was the most testing part of the course, was left until the final term, Firth maintained that it was a subject in 'which the student must rely chiefly on himself'. It was left until the end of the course because that was the point when the student, having learned to read, take notes and arrange his thoughts, could use his time most constructively. The most popular of the six subjects offered, were 'The French Revolution', 'The Great Rebellion', 'Italy, 1492–1513' and 'India, 1773–1805'. The reading for each one was equally voluminous. But some subjects were perhaps less arduous than others, particularly those which did not require a foreign language. Despite Firth's warning that the student would have to work on his own, classes were offered by Lodge on the French Revolution, Fletcher on the Great Rebellion, and J. H. Maude of Hertford on Hildebrand.[42]

While keeping up with his reading and attending the half-dozen or so lectures the student had also to write a weekly essay for his college tutor. Essay reading became a regular part of the history tutor's job in the 1870s. The men were asked to pay particular attention to one aspect of their current study, extra reading was prescribed, and questions arising from the reading were then set for essays. It was one means of a college maintaining a form of disciplinary control over its own students while at the same time monitoring their academic progress. The duties of the history tutor at Trinity were that he 'takes all the men for that school, and sees that they go to the proper lectures, and himself takes them in Essays'. Though Charles Oman boasted that he never once wrote a weekly essay, he was undoubtedly an exception. When he became tutor at New College he had twenty-five pupils and saw each one privately every week during term to criticise their essays.[43]

In theory, then, the student had to work hard at his course. But in practice what was the relationship between reading and lectures? What, through the essay, did the tutor encourage and develop in the student, and what was the relationship between teaching and examinations?

Firth warned unsuspecting students, 'you will have to read really hard'. Superficially, at least, the length of the book lists prescribed would seem to validate his warning. Teachers both inside and outside the School of History commented upon the 'vast number of books to be either consulted or read'. Matthew Arnold declared that he did 'not like the course for the History school at all; nothing but read, read, read, endless histories'. One anonymous teacher said that he could do little but 'despair of the possibility of ever wading through such a mass'.[44]

Nevertheless the drawing up of the book lists involved a certain amount of doublespeak. Paul Fredericq made the telling point that 'As a bibliographic index it is perfect'. He was right. For that is what it was intended to be. It was part of the History School's answer to critics who doubted that it was 'substantive enough to furnish the training for a class examination of a high character'. The lists were intended to show that the good history student was as learned and as well read as the best classic. Firth's warning was just one part of a scarecrow flysheet intended to frighten away any stray students who believed the School of History to be a rich harvest of easy pickings. Fredericq posed the rhetorical question, 'But is it possible for the student to read all these books? Evidently not, for care is often taken to indicate chapters and even the pages to be referred to.' Students were indeed directed to particular sections of certain works. But while the book lists were by no means as fearsome as they at first sight appeared, Fredericq's remark that 'The science is thus chalked out' was also wide of the mark. The amount of reading, if not overwhelming, was still substantial and it had to be related to the syllabus. Students could afford little time to read around their subject. This was where lectures made their impact.[45]

Charles Oman entered the History School full of confidence in 1878. He was well read and, at a time when few schools taught history, certainly much better prepared than most of his fellow students. Realising that his knowledge of English political history was probably good, Oman's tutor told him that in his first year he would have most difficulty with the constitutional history paper. It contained a great deal of technical detail of which the general reader was ignorant. In this, confided Oman:

George was absolutely right, I had always read history either as illustrating archaeology, or else as romance – the story of the heroes and the villains of all the ages. To consider it as a process of constitutional evolution was rather a new idea to me.

It was new to most students, and made the more difficult by the fact that they were required to support their work with close reference to the original documents printed in Stubbs's *Charters*. Even in 1879 the Charters had 'already become a sort of bible, from which a candidate was expected to identify any paragraph without its context being given'. It was a text which had to be not only mastered but assimilated with the rest of a student's reading on the subject. In this, said Oman:

> I was helped . . . by the one series of lectures which I attended that year, the 'Steps to Stubbs' as they were called of A. L. Smith of Balliol . . . One needed some guidance as to what part of the 'Charters' were of primary importance, for the book itself gave no help towards the sifting out of the crucial passages. . . . And the mere translation was hard enough, for the book lacked a sufficient explanatory vocabulary of technical terms at the end.[46]

A summary of the lectures which Oman praised survive in booklet form. They are a brilliant analytical synthesis of Stubbs's *Charters*. Unlike Stubbs, who arranged the printed documents in chronological order, Smith organised his analysis of them according to their content and subject matter. His booklet was divided into topics upon which the student might be expected to comment. Around each topic was drawn all the relevant information, and from it a pattern of development was formed. In this manner the Church, the Crown, the administrative system, the baronage, social divisions, military systems, Parliament and taxation were all ticketed and presented to the student complete with illustrations from, and further references to, not only Stubbs's *Charters* but other original printed documents.[47]

The lectures are thorough, detailed, and a model of clarity. Presentation was a chief feature of Smith's teaching. It is illustrated further by his lecture course on constitutional history to which the 'Steps the Stubbs' was a detailed appendix. Once again the subject was reduced to manageable proportions and tackled small step by small step. Smith's lectures are based almost entirely upon printed or secondary sources, the same sources to which the student himself was directed. They involve a thorough criticism of historical works. Thus in Lecture II of the series, entitled 'The Making of England', Smith set out to discuss the question of racial intermixture following the Teutonic invasions and asked the question, 'How far were the conquered Celts allowed to survive? He then outlined carefully the contrasting answers to the question, indicating in some detail the evidence available to historians. This was followed by a long and detailed analysis of Seebohm's continuity theory.[48]

Smith's lectures were designed to provide the student with three things. They divided the course into manageable sections upon which the student could concentrate and build without becoming lost or confused; as well as analysis of the historical process they provided him with a detailed factual framework upon which he could base further reading and graft further details. And they offered the student a guide to and criticism of the relevant literature on the subject.

Smith's aims were reflected by other college tutors. C. W. Boase was one of the first teachers of modern history in Oxford. He was also one of the most respected.[49] Like Smith he published little. But like Smith he made teaching a career, and his lectures encompass the same, very definite aims. Boase lectured on the history of early modern Europe. His first task was to define, and then to break the period down. 'In the sixteenth century', he told his classes:

> Europe passed through a great crisis, the Middle Ages came to an end, modern history began. The new faith strove against the old, national and municipal freedom against despotism, the feudal nobles against the central government.[50]

And further:

> When Henry won the battle of Bosworth in 1485, . . . our country was still in great measure under the regime of feudalism; when Elizabeth died in 1603, it had passed into the England which we know. Some writers tell us that there is no break in History, that all is continuous development; and, in a sense this is true: but if the spirit is the life, then this is not true: for the spirit of Classical times differed essentially from that of the Middle Ages, as this again did from that of Modern Times.[51]

Boase broke history into periods, and periods into small compact and manageable portions. But each period was invested with significance in relation to the whole. He dealt with national politics, given life through the agency of kings and statesmen. Judgement on political figures was made entirely in relation to their ultimate success or failure in terms of national development. Thus:

> England had gladly for the time [endured] a temporary dictatorship. England knew its rulers and . . . those rulers knew England . . . Henry VI was well fitted for his part of the work. . . . He kept England out of continental war and gave it time to grow.[52]

> Elizabeth died 3 April 1603. Her contemporaries recognised her services to Europe. Without her, Philip II would perhaps have, at least for a time, won the day. But the great Queen was dead, and James I reigned in her stead, a man of no little ability in some respects, with learning enough for a school master, and theology enough for a bishop, but woefully deficient in kingcraft.[53]

Boase offered more than a simple analysis. In most of his lectures the narrative is very detailed. There were few comprehensive text-books and Boase's lectures were, in part, intended to remedy the deficiency. But like Smith he took his lecture notes from secondary sources, all of which were available and recommended to students. Like Smith, he was guiding his students through the book list and providing the basic minimum amount of information upon which further studies could be based.

Teaching history became as much an art as the writing of it. Good tutors became influential. It is one of the great anomalies of the Oxford History School that Johnson and A. L. Smith's classes on the 'Steps to Stubbs' were packed, while Stubbs himself, lecturing on 'Constitutional History', professed himself disappointed with the size of his audience.

When lecturers found a successful system they repeated it. Lecturing became a matter of routine. The notes of Boase, Smith and Lodge are instructive in this respect. One page of Boase's course on 'Early Constitutional History' bears minor marks of revision dated 21 October 1880, 26 April 1882, 18 October 1883, 22 October 1885, 20 January 1887. There are few factual alterations and only two instances of extra detail being appended to the text. He delivered the same lecture over a period of seven years.[54]

Smith and Lodge's notes reveal a similar pattern, though they are indicative of a further stage in the teaching process. Smith was a great pioneer. He did much to raise standards. K. N. Bell said that he was the greatest tutor of his time, H. W. C. Davis that he 'founded a school of teachers who were profoundly influenced by his precept and example.'[55] His lecture notes are impressive. Arranged in neat, comprehensible divisions, points clearly marked, they are a model of simplicity. Having made the subject of constitutional history his own, Smith began to print his lecture courses, and to present students with copies, complete with bibliographic references. Balliol College has two complete copies of these handouts, the first dated 1889–90, the second 1893. They are identical. It is not easy to say quite when Smith began printing his lectures or for how long the process continued, but clearly both information and structure remained constant over a number of years. Once he found a system, he stuck to it.[56]

While lectures and reading provided the information necessary to pass examinations the student had to learn to convey that knowledge quickly and precisely. This skill was developed through the writing of weekly essays. W. J. Ashley outlined the technique of essay writing. Authors must be read and abstracted. Ideas must be noted and then ordered logically. Essays must be concise. There must be no extraneous detail. Quite simply 'the salvation of an essay is "point" '. Fine writing and waffle were to be avoided at all costs. A story told of A. L. Smith illustrates Ashley's last point. A student attended one of Smith's supervisions, bearing a sheaf of extra notes. 'Are those extracts in your essay?' demanded Smith. 'Well, either they are in your essay or they are not. If they are, read them. If they are not, we don't want them.' For the purposes of examination, knowledge was wasted unless put down on paper and there applied direct to the question. His wife's view that 'he made men seek essentials and try to write about them tersely, forcibly and logically' is certainly borne out by essays written for him.[57]

One such essay, 'Does Machiavelli succeed in his attempt to separate Politics from Morals?' by K. M. Thomas of Lady Margaret Hall, was passed by her tutor. It is only 1,200 words long. There are few quotations from the text, and none from the critics. The essay is direct, the points are succinct. Smith made but two comments. One was that on the question of public and private ethics a comparison could be made with Treitschke, and the second was a sharp admonition of a burst of emotion issued with respect to Machiavelli's 'persistent use of immoral means'.[58]

The technique which tutors encouraged in the essay question was the only method by which success could be gained in the examination. Students were faced with long and demanding question papers of which they must complete as much as they could. There was little time for fine writing or surplus detail. A chance survival has accorded us a unique opportunity to see how closely one student followed his tutor's advice in composing essay answers to examination questions.

Among the leaves of one of C. W. Boase's many notebooks an examination script has lain buried for over a hundred years. Why he kept a script which he ought to have destroyed is a matter of conjecture. It is possible that the candidate was one of his own pupils. We do not know, because the name has been torn out. The candidate was by no means best of his year. His paper was assessed as a high Second, not a First Class standard. One answer suggests itself. This particular paper – the 'Constitutional and Political Paper' of 1873 – was the first of the restructured school. Boase was examiner. He and his colleagues had to set new standards of achievement in a new discipline. It is possible that he kept one paper for reference. It was a good Second – not quite top-class, but deserving of merit. The script may have been used to set levels of attainment.

The candidate was faced with twelve broad-ranging questions. He had to complete what he could in three hours. Historians have been puzzled by examination requirements, and much astonishment has been expressed at the magnitude of the task confronting students. For the first time we are able to assess it accurately. One thing is immediately clear. Students did not have to answer all the questions. Unlike those of the 1850s, answers were expected to be thorough, and to take the form of essay compositions. Our candidate who, we may recall, was above average standard, answered six questions – four thoroughly, and two partially. He completed eighteen sides of quarto paper in the process of writing answers to questions (i) (five sides), (ii) (three sides), (v) (five sides), (vii) (three sides), (ix) (one

side) and (xii) (one side). Quantity has obviously a tenuous relationship with quality where answers to questions are concerned, but
a little discernment shows that the last two questions were rushed
and incomplete. The student was placed in an awkward situation.
He had to complete enough questions to impress upon the examiners his breadth of knowledge, yet his answers must be detailed
enough to meet the requirements of the question. This is where the
method of practising essay questions was so important. All the
examination questions bar the last, and to some extent numbers
three, seven and ten, were designed to elicit succinct answers.

Our candidate's answers were most direct. They reflect the lessons which tutors taught their pupils. In question

(2) Explain the constitutional difficulties which have arisen from the fact
that William III and the kings of the house of Brunswick possessed large
continental dominions. Can you illustrate this from earlier English
History?

and question

(7) How did the religious reformation of the sixteenth century affect the
development of political theory throughout Europe?

the opportunity for digression is vast, but the answers are succinct.
The candidate began and finished his questions abruptly. There is no
long introduction and no conclusion. Points are ordered logically
and related directly to the question. Thus for question (7), for
instance, the first sentence reads, 'The first effect of the Reformation
in those countries where it prevailed was to overthrow or greatly
limit the vast powers of the clergy. . . .' As Smith told his pupils, there
was no time for waffle or literary chaff. Time was short and answers
must be to the point. Thus our candidate continued in question (7)
to say that:

It is necessary in estimating the political influence of the Reformation to
realise the fact that beside the overshadowing Papal influence which
boasted of a supremacy over all temporal sovereigns, the clergy, as, up to
the Fifteenth Century the sole possessors of a liberal education or what
passed for it, were possessed almost exclusively of the administrative
power in Christian countries; they had also in the wealth of their chief
prelates and monasteries a material power equal to that of the nobles and

constituting them, along with their vast spiritual power and the possession of the administration, by far the most prominent feature in all
politics. They embraced or were supreme in the professions of law and
physic. . . .

The length of sentence is an indication of flowing thought. It is by
no means a model of perfect grammar, but it shows a mind working
quickly under pressure, grouping and linking related points under a
definite heading. Our candidate then proceeded to discuss briefly
the shift in the balance of power between the three estates which he
maintained resulted from the Reformation. The Reformation, he
said, 'pointed to the distinction of lay and secular authority, a principle which has grown in strength ever since'. This was his main
contention, and he briefly identified other changes which resulted
from it:

> the legal profession grew, and occupied afterwards all legal offices of
> authority before attached to the church, except for a short period when
> Laud was supreme in the counsel of Charles I . . . Education had now
> spread, so that in England and abroad the nobles were competent to
> direct administration . . . men began to question all privileges. . . .

The answer is dogmatic. There is little weighing of opinion; there
are, as in the essay written for Smith, no references to sources, not
even secondary sources, and no quotations. The candidate was
answering a question rather than displaying evidence of extensive or
deep reading in a given subject. Furthermore, he did not attempt to
answer above half the questions on the paper, yet he took a good
Second. The examiners awarded his class on the basis of an ability to
think quickly and clearly, and to marshal evidence in support of his
answers. As with the scripts written at Cambridge for Sir James
Stephen, the examiners at Oxford took into account both quantity
and quality when determining a candidate's class.[59]

The nature of lectures and the relationship they bore to specified
reading, and the drilling of candidates by tutors in the technique of
writing examination questions, leads us to the subject most hotly
debated outside the School. While lectures covered the scope of the
syllabus upon which examination papers were based, how closely
did they correspond to the questions which were set?

As early as 1873 Montagu Burrows suggested that answers to

examination papers 'are not now so much derived from standard books as from lectures'. In 1877 he went further. Tutors, he claimed, had prejudiced any chance the professors might have of securing an audience because they taught 'simply in the subjects of the examination, with reference to the examination papers, and obtaining honours in the examination'. Stubbs agreed and accepted the fact. Had not Oman listened to lectures by Smith on Stubbs on the constitution? Max Müller suggested that:

> the sole object of a student at Oxford is to take a high class . . . it does not pay to look beyond a given narrow horizon . . . to look beyond that teaching which is supplied in college lectures, and the results of which he is expected to produce before the examiners, most of whom are again tutors in the different colleges of the university.[60]

Müller's accusations were ignored. Their overtones lay buried deep between the covers of a large report. Though he was not alone in his condemnation that tutors were securing their livelihood by 'spoon-feeding' candidates with information which paid in examinations and, further, by regulating the examination system and setting its standards, a serious challenge was not forthcoming until 1889, when J. E. T. Rogers produced a stinging denunciation of the School of Modern History.

Rogers's article is bitter and resentful. It is aimed less at the School than at college tutors and their self-appointed role as educators. Rogers denied them that function. As a class, he claimed, they were second-rate men of diminished intellect, who, in despair of finding gainful employment elsewhere, had perpetrated the myth that they were training a rising generation. Rogers implied that they had achieved their goal by creating a monopoly of the power to teach and examine. The link between the two roles was incestuous and forged through the widespread dispensation in lectures of 'salvation knowledge'. He suggested that, when examining, tutors exercised regularly an 'unconscious favouritism', and this in a subject which already left open too much room for 'speculative opinion'. Rogers left no one in doubt of his implications. Oxford history teachers simply claimed and exercised the power to 'ticket' their pupils for life.[61]

Rogers was extreme. His last point about the marking of scripts was untrue. College tutors who were designated examiners could not see scripts written by men from their own college. External examiners were appointed to maintain standards and see that they were consistent over a period of years. As S. R. Gardiner noted, the examination could not be conducted without internal examiners who were aware of the content of the syllabus and the amount of knowledge which would reasonably be expected of the candidate.[62] But one point still remained. How closely did lectures correspond with examinations? Were students simply crammed with information which would ease them through the examination with the least possible effort?

We have seen that lectures were well organised and that in them the student was fed a good deal of information. Indeed, the examination script on occasions contains more than a hint that the candidate was repeating the sort of platitudes which Boase included in his lectures:

> All political speculation since the reformation, setting aside the interested and pedantic James I, and the prejudiced writings of such extreme royalists as Hobbes and Sir R. Filmer has been towards grounding authority upon free contract, not as universally in pre-reformation times upon Divine ordinance.

on p. 16 of the script being one such example. It is less than likely that the candidate was familiar with the content of 'all political speculation since the reformation', and his loose generalisation is the sort he might have noted from one of his lecturers.

It also seems likely that most students expected information which paid in examinations. One of Tout's ex-students wrote to him from Oxford about his performance in the Schools. He had taken a Second, and with it his prospects of employment as a lecturer in one of the new university colleges had receded dramatically. The student blamed his misfortune on a combination of incidents in which bad luck and the fickle hand of fate predominated over bad management and lack of industry. Nevertheless he told Tout that:

> I have an additional cause for complaint in that I had expected that Mr. Firth's lectures would have been useful to me; for I devoted special attention to them to the comparative exclusion of my own abstracts. I spent Thursday night till about 4 a.m. cramming piles of Mr. Firth's

lectures on the 'characteristics', the 'omissions' ... etc. in Clarendon
Cromwell, Baillee and Ludlow, with most disastrous results. Nothing I
read was of any use on the questions set, and if Mr. Firth set the papers he
seems systematically to have avoided his own lectures.

Mr Roberts's note would doubtless have produced a gleeful smile
from Mr Firth, who was later to make a public point of teaching what
he rather than the examiners felt to be interesting and important.
Firth's pleasure would have been enhanced, however, if he could
have compared his own review with that of other lecturers:

> Mr. Hassall's lectures – a course I attended two years ago on Louis XIV,
> and a few I went to lately on the Tudor period paid admirably in the later
> Foreign and in the General Political paper – both evidently set by him.[63]

But does the fact that students expected their lectures to pay add
fuel to Rogers's accusations? At first glance it would seem that
Hassall might have been guilty of the sort of crimes which Rogers
suggested were commonplace. Nevertheless the role of the lecturer
was a difficult one. Most students were strangers to historical study.
They had but two years in which to complete an extensive course.
Lectures – particularly core course lectures – were an introduction to
the subject which prevented the student from becoming lost in his
reading. As both Boase's and Lodge's lectures show, they were
intended to provide the student with enough information for him to
construct an intelligible narrative of events. Some lectures provided
a little more than that, and some a little less. Equally, however, some
students completed a good deal of extra reading and some less than
enough. Roberts was a Second Class man, one who by his own
testimony averaged B– and B+ grades – one who was on a par with
our candidate who wrote the examination script. Roberts believed
that he had been 'particularly unfortunate in the papers', suggesting
that his favourite topics had not come up. Indeed, in three papers he
took γ grades. He was asked questions in his viva which he could
not answer. On some subjects he had not completed enough
reading around his lectures, and was therefore stamped like our
earlier candidate as a Second Class man.[64]

There is a subtle difference between a well structured, well
organised course of lectures which covered the syllabus, and direct
cramming for the purposes of examination. Rogers's accusations

will stand up only if a direct correlation can be drawn between lectures and examination questions.

In Hassall's case it seems that such a correlation may have been possible. In the case of Firth it was not, and where Boase, Smith and Lodge were concerned it seems unlikely. They used very much the same notes and delivered very much the same lectures year in, year out. Yet, while lectures did not vary substantially, examiners and the questions they set did. Neither Smith's, nor Boase's, nor Lodge's lectures bear any consistently direct relationship to examination papers. This is not to say that students would not find them useful. Smith's masterly division of subject matter would have been an undoubted advantage to students reading constitutional history. His subdivision of the Charters would help the student to recognise the gobbets, and in some cases questions could almost be answered from printed notes, but even in these instances the student would have had to have done the recommended reading to which the lecturer had directed him.

Burrows, Müller and Rogers were critical of a system which tended to pre-empt their own influence as teachers. Examinations dominated the student's life. Most college teachers respected the system under which they taught. They geared their efforts to the syllabus, and covered that syllabus thoroughly. But this some professors refused to do, and by so doing put themselves in the position of Vaughan some thirty years earlier. Colleges and students wanted results. The ambitious student had little time for the professor who taught what he did not need to know. The argument engendered by Rogers serves simply to illustrate the great division of function which had emerged between the professional teacher and the professor whose quasi-formal duties included research. The teachers were doing their job efficiently. But already, within twenty years of the foundation of the independent School, there was concern that the history student's course was not searching enough, and that the division of function between tutor and professor was based upon a false conception of what constituted an adequate historical education.

NOTES TO CHAPTER 6

1   Heyck, The Transformation of Intellectual Life, pp. 144–5. Marwick, The Nature of History, p. 46. Southern, The Shape and Substance of Academic History, p. 411.

2   J. J. Hooper, The establishment of a School of Jurisprudence in the University of Oxford (London, 1854). Travers Twiss, A Letter to the Vice Chancellor of the University of Oxford, on the Law Studies of the University (London, 1859). Charles Neate, Remarks on Legal and other Studies of the University (Oxford, 1856).

3   M. Bernard, A Letter to the Vice Chancellor on the Provision for the Teaching of Law at Oxford (London, 1864), p. 8. See also C. S. Roundell, The following Letter to the Vice Chancellor is circulated at the Request of the Hebdomadal Council (Oxford, 1864).

4   E. A. Freeman, 'Historical study at Oxford', Bentley's Quarterly Review, 1, 1859, 282–300 (p. 292).

5   Oxford University Gazette, 1, No. 9, Tuesday 22 March 1870, p. 6.

6   Special Report from the Select Committee on the Oxford and Cambridge Universities Education Bill . . . 31 July 1867, para. 2292.

7   Special Report, para. 1448.

8   New College, Archives, Minutes of the Warden and Tutors' Meetings, 1866–82, Min. 23 January 1866 (p. 2). See also 25 January 1868.

9   Heyck, The Transformation of Intellectual Life, p. 148.

10   Minutes of Evidence taken by the University of Oxford Commissioners . . ., 1881, para. 1337.

11   New College Archives, Minutes of the Warden and Tutors' Meetings, 10 November 1869, p. 106.

12   Gazette, 1, No. 2, Tuesday 11 February 1870, p. 12.

13   Stubbs, Seventeen Lectures, p. 110.

14   Stubbs, Seventeen Lectures, p. 39.

15   Stubbs, Seventeen Lectures, p. 17.

16   W. J. Ashley, 'Modern History at Oxford', in European Schools of History and Politics, ed. A. D. White, Johns Hopkins Studies in Historical and Political Science, Fifth Series, 12, 1887, pp. 45–66 (p. 48).

17   Bodleian Library, O.U.A. MH/M/1/1 Minutes, 25 October 1883 (p. 15). 11 December 1883 (pp. 25–6).

18   Ashley, 'Modern history', p. 48.

19   Oxford University Examination Papers, Trinity Term, 1885.

20   Oxford University Examination Papers, Trinity Term, 1885.

21   Minutes of Evidence . . . 1881, para. 2847. Stubbs, Seventeen Lectures, p. 83, p. 112.

22   Bodleian Library, O.U.A. MH/M/1/1/1 February 1884, pp. 28–33. A. L. Smith, 'The new History School', Oxford Magazine, vol. 4, 10 February 1886, 36–7 (p. 36).

23   J.W.C., 'The new History School', Oxford Magazine, 4, 17 February 1886, p. 64.

24   Minutes of Evidence . . . 1881, para. 1395.

25   See the papers of C. W. Boase, who lectured in history at Exeter College (where the papers are collected) from 1852 to 1895. For catechetical lectures see Exeter College Archives J.1.20, J.1.14, J.11.4. These continued in part with Stubbs's Charters (J.1.6) and J.11.2 but sixteen sets of wider notes show the extent of the change in style.

26   These being according to Boase, Minutes of Evidence, para. 1253, and George, para. 4506; Worcester and Hertford but see also Merton Collge, Oxford, Archives P/2/17, which claims they were Worcester and Pembroke.

27   New College, Archives, 2233, Regulations relating to Undergraduate Members of The College, October 1884, and Minutes of the Warden and Tutors' meetings, 1866–82, 18 March 1867, 'Mr. Cripps having absented himself without sufficient reason from Mr. Newman's lectures was desired to make an analysis of those parts of Hallam's Middle Ages and Lingard's History of England in which Mr. Newman had been lecturing during the Term, and to bring it to his Tutor by Saturday May 11th and was warned that any disregard in future of College rules . . . would be brought before the College as a serious breach of discipline.'

28 Minutes of Evidence, para. 1269, para. 4512, Merton College, P/2/17, Evidence of R. W. Roper.
29 C. H. Firth, The Faculties and their Powers (Oxford, 1909).
30 Minutes of Evidence, para. 754, para. 756. Stubbs, Seventeen Lectures, pp. 35–6.
31 Minutes of Evidence, paras. 1280–327 (1286, 1321, 1323, 1324, 1325).
32 E. A. Freeman, 'Oxford after forty years', Contemporary Review, 51, 1887, 609–23, 814–30.
33 New College, D.380, Letter of Enquiry sent by the Vice-Chancellor (Oxford, May 1874), pp. 38–44 (p. 39).
34 Firth, The Faculties and their Powers, p. 12. Freeman, 'Oxford after forty years', p. 622.
35 Minutes of Evidence, para. 2379.
36 Minutes of Evidence, para. 1351–2 (1351).
37 John Higham, 'The historical profession', in History: the Development of Historical Studies in the United States, by John Higham, with Leonard Krieger and Felix Gilbert (New Jersey, 1965), pp. 1–86 (p. 5).
38 Heyck, The Transformation of Intellectual Life, pp. 155–86.
39 Felix Gilbert, 'European and American historiography', in Higham et al., History . . ., pp. 315–88 (335–7).
40 Mary Smith, Arthur Lionel Smith, Master of Balliol, 1916–1924: a Biography and some Reminiscences by his wife (London, 1928), p. 87. For an excellent account of academic consciousness in Oxford see Arthur Engel, From Clergyman to Don: the Rise of the Academic Profession in Nineteenth-century Oxford (Oxford, 1983).
41 Emmanuel College, col. 9.39b.212, Gwatkin to Creighton, 14 June 1891, 'you are more a writer, I more a teacher; and I must lay my plans accordingly'. R. H. S. Prothero, p. 2/1/10, Testimonials, Edinburgh. 'The duties of this post, involving a general supervision of the educational work of the College, are too onerous to leave much time for original research or important literary work.'
42 W. J. Ashley, 'Modern history at Oxford', p. 48, p. 49, p. 52. Bodleian, GA Oxon. b.140, C. H. Firth, Honour School of Modern History (March 1886). Gazette, vol. XVII, 1886–87, 18 October 1886, p. 36, 17 January 1887, p. 220, 25 April 1887, p. 374, 18 October 1887, p. 52; vol. XVIII, 1887–88, 16 January 1888, p. 244. Minutes of Evidence, paras. 2843–2845.
43 Merton College, Archives, P/2/17, R. W. Roper. Minutes of Evidence, para. 1292. C. W. C. Oman, Memories of Victorian Oxford (London, 1941), p. 94, p. 148.
44 Fredericq, The Study of History, p. 36. The Letters of Matthew Arnold, 1848–88 (in two volumes), ed. G. W. E. Russell (London, 1895), second edition, vol. II, p. 142. J.W.C., 'The new History School', p. 64. Firth, Honours School, p. 3.
45 Fredericq, The Study of History pp. 39, 40. Firth, Honours in History (Oxford, 1903).
46 Oman, Memories, pp. 104–5.
47 Balliol College, MS. Collection. A. L. Smith, Papers, Section 1, Box 5.
48 Balliol College, Pamphlet Collection, A. L. Smith, English Constitutional History from the Beginning to 1307.
49 See Stubbs, Seventeen Lectures (third edition, 1900), p. ix.
50 Exeter College, Archives, College History, Box 6, L.11.7, The Sixteenth century, fol. 4, 1610–1715, Lecture II, 24 January 1884.
51 Exeter College, Archives, C.H., Box 5, L.11.6, The Tudors, fol. 1.
52 Exeter College, Archives, L.11.6, The Tudors, fol. 2–3.
53 Exeter College, Archives, L.11.7, European History, 1600–1715, fol. 6 (27 October 1886).
54 Exeter College, Archives, L.11.7, Constitutional History, fol. 3.
55 M. Smith, Arthur Lionel Smith, p. 305, p. 284.
56 Balliol College MS. Collection. Compiled by O. Wardrof and E. A. MacCurdy.
57 W. J. Ashley, 'Modern History at Oxford', pp. 52–3 (p. 53). M. Smith, Arthur Lionel Smith p. 218.

E

58   Ealliol College, MS. Collection A. L. Smith Papers, Section II, Box 3.
59   Exeter College, Archives, C. W. Boase Papers, J.I.8. I discovered the paper among the leaves of one of Boase's notebooks, where it had lain, apparently untouched, since his death. For a copy see Slee, *History as a Discipline*, Appendix II.
60   New College, D.380, p. 42. *Minutes of Evidence* para. 754, 1228, 4115 (3885). Merton College, P/2/17, W. Wallace, 18 November 1881. Stubbs, *Seventeen Lectures*, p. 36.
61   J. E. T. Rogers, 'Oxford Professors and Oxford tutors', *Contemporary Review*, LVI, 1889, 926–36.
62   S. R. Gardiner, M. Creighton, W. Hunt, E. S. Beesley, T. F. Tout, A. H. Johnson, E. Armstrong, A. L. Smith and R. Lodge, 'Oxford professors and Oxford tutors; reply of the examiners in the school of Modern History', *Contemporary Review*, LVII, 1890, 183–86.
63   John Rylands University Library of Manchester, Papers of T. F. Tout, 1/1021/15, L. J. Roberts to T. F. Tout, 12 June 1892.
64   J.R.U.L.M. Tout, 1/1021/15–16. Roberts to Tout, June 12 1892, July 20 1892.

PART THREE

A liberal education
or a
training in research?

CHAPTER 7

'An endeavour to train men capable of adding to knowledge'
BURY, FIRTH AND TOUT
– THE NEW SCHOOL

From the mid-1880s the role of history as an academic discipline was agreed upon widely by teachers of the subject at most institutions of higher education. George Prothero noted that history had achieved independent academic status through 'the recognition of a new principle in education – the principle ... that every great subject, if seriously and methodically taught, affords good training for the mind, nay more, is especially fitted for certain minds'. History was taught and studied as one avenue to the ideal goal of a liberal education.[1]

In the 1880s, however, the value of a liberal education was challenged. Britain was struggling in the down-cycle of a severe economic recession. Influential opinion suggested that economic and social collapse could be prevented only by direct State intervention. A Royal Commission was appointed to uncover the truth of the matter. Was Britain really in the grip of a depression? If so, what was causing it, and how could the trend be reversed? The commission reported in 1886. The situation was indeed serious. Staple industries – iron, coal, cotton – were in decline. Prices were falling while wages had risen considerably, leaving profits at their lowest for many years. Unemployment among the unskilled had reached chronic levels and seemed certain to get worse. Some claimed Britain was overproducing. But that was not the answer. Industrial output had simply kept pace with the overall growth in world trade. But Britain's share of the world market had fallen drastically. The root cause of the depression was that she could not compete effectively with her trade rivals. The Germans, the French, the Americans produced goods of better quality more cheaply. They kept prices down by establishing protective tariffs, tax incentives and better labour relations. But superior quality was the product of better design and a more efficient production process. It was clear that British industry was becoming increasingly outmoded. Britain was deficient in high tech. Unlike her competitors she had failed notably to harness intellectual resources to the industrial process. Her education system was not geared to improve national productivity. The solution was clear. The commissioners stated it plainly. 'We shall only be able to hold our ground by a continual advance in intellectual training, scientific knowledge and true artistic taste on the part of both employers and workmen.' A programme of manpower planning was required. A new generation of technologists and technicians must be trained to help the country face the future on its own terms. Universities must respond by investing a much greater proportion of their resources in science and technology.[2]

The universities responded in kind. They began by explaining that national efficiency was a complex business. Economic success did not rest solely on the appliance of science. Products must be sold. Markets had to be defined, explored, captured and protected. Goods must be advertised, distributed and bought. The work force needed managing, placating and above all educating. Politicians, soldiers, accountants, lawyers, advertisers, entrepreneurs, teachers, managers, civil servants and welfare workers all had their part to play in the social and economic revival. Some, it was true, could be trained directly for the job. But others, equally, could not. One thing was clear. Tomorrow's technocrats must be flexible. They must be capable of analysing, understanding and adapting successfully to changing circumstances. The key to Britain's revival lay in mental regeneration; in the creation of a reservoir of 'skilled brainpower.' This could be developed only by a general and widespread programme of academic studies – by a liberal education, in fact.

It was an impressive claim. But it did not rest there. Within this general framework practitioners of developing disciplines –

economics, history, languages – were keen to demonstrate the specific utility of their own particular study. They did it naturally and without a trace of self-consciousness. Financial pressures made sales talk an integral part of their job. Bar the largest Oxbridge colleges, all institutions of higher education were run to tight budgets. They relied on two sources of income – private donation and student fees. The whim of the benefactor was unpredictable, and while not completely beyond the power of suggestion it often bore little relation to the needs of a balanced curriculum. But in the pre-grant age students had to be wooed. A considerable investment was made in their education. Few could afford to take the decision lightly. Many took it with a view to maximising their career prospects – be it at the bar, in the army, the civil service, the Church or in teaching. Quite simply academics were forced by straightened circumstances to think hard about the value and purpose of higher education and plan accordingly. To obtain classes, to maintain a viable department, often to make a living, they had to convince consumers that their investment in education was likely to be worth while. Alfred Marshall, W. J. Ashley and Henry Sidgwick, among others, were unstinting in their efforts to explain in clear and simple terms the methods and means by which their own discipline could add to a student's marketable value.[3]

Teachers of history were no exception. They were equally keen to promote the practical benefits of historical study and to stress the unique value of its currency among the forces of the market place. In doing so they trod the narrowest of lines. That the universities had a service role none denied. But it was clear that it would best be upheld by adhering rigidly to strict academic values. The creative, flexible intelligence the nation required so desperately was fostered not by the assimilation of useful technical information but by a rigorous training of the mind. The emphasis was on process and method. Historical subject matter was cherished mainly as a vehicle for developing transferable skills. It was the way the mind responded to the challenges presented by the subject matter that was of primary importance. History was neither a dry, irrelevant academic subject nor a narrow, technical directly vocational pursuit. Its scope was wide-ranging and flexible, for besides providing the basis of active and responsible citizenship it was a useful preliminary training for intending journalists, civil servants, lawyers, politicians and teachers. One thing was clear. To be most valuable the subject must be left to follow the contours of science.[4]

The university history schools claimed a good deal of success, both in attracting students and in training them to take their place among the 'expanding' 'middle' and 'upper-middle' class professions.[5] At Oxford in the period 1890–94 an average 104 men a year graduated with Honours in history. Only Literae Humaniores attracted more. At Cambridge the school was smaller. Over the same period twenty-six men on average graduated each year in history. While the History School was much smaller than that of Mathematics, Natural Science and Classics, and on a par with Law and Theology, it was growing much faster than any of them. By 1914 history at Cambridge, like history at Oxford, was the most popular Honours school.

But what did history graduates do in 'after-life'? Research currently being undertaken in Oxford by the History of Oxford University Project suggests strongly that from the middle 1890s Oxford history graduates joined the professions. Of those who matriculated in the late 1890s some 25% went into the Church, 15% into the legal profession, approximately 17% into teaching either at school or at university, 9% into politics, the civil service and local government, and another 6% into banking and commerce. Deborah Wormell has conducted a survey of the careers of Cambridge students who took a First or Second Class degree in history between 1872 and 1895. An accurate comparison with the Oxford figures is not possible, but she discovered that while 18·1% of Cambridge history graduates went into government or public administration and 17·1% became teachers of history in colleges or universities (proportions which would undoubtedly be much lower, were the Third Class students considered); most 'followed the traditional graduate professions of law, the ministry, schoolteaching and social work'. Clearly a history degree did not disqualify a man from seeking a niche in one of the expanding professions. But without more detailed information about the correlation between social background, academic results and occupational status we cannot evaluate with any accuracy the claims of the history teachers that they trained a rising generation. Evidence generated by the History of Oxford University Project on career patterns of Oxford graduates suggests that those who had studied history were little different from the average. There does seem to be some social mobility among Oxford undergraduates. In the period 1878–98 there is evidence to suggest that the sons of landowners and clergymen looked outside their fathers' occupations for employment. A similar though less well defined trend is evident among some of the business and commercial classes. But most of the movement appears to be lateral and within professional sub-groups, lending cogency to the argument of Jenkins and Caradog Jones that the future careers of university graduates depended on an unstable mixture of academic and social credentialism, and perhaps lending some weight to Professor Banks's view that education was becoming a necessary means of maintaining one's social position or, if a second son, at least a means of securing a reasonable start in life.[6]

Most Cambridge men (though by no means all) believed that Oxford led the way in historical education, and most Oxford men (though by no means all) agreed.[7] But from 1885 the difference between the two Schools was not great. As a general consensus was reached about the ends of higher education and the ideal format of an historical education, so the syllabus at both universities grew to be similar. The Oxbridge student received a thorough grounding in English political and constitutional history. He acquired a rudimentary knowledge of the chief cognate sciences in which reasoning was based on historical data, and he undertook the detailed study of a special subject which was conducted in the original authorities.

There were differences. As a by-product of its own historical antecedents – a long connection with the Moral Sciences Tripos, a shortage of teaching staff, and Seeley's influence – the Cambridge curriculum placed greater emphasis on the theoretical subjects, particularly on political science. Through the persistence of Cunningham economic history was given greater prominence at Cambridge than at Oxford. Oxford students expended greater effort on constitutional history and were also taught European history, the lack of which was considered the most serious defect of the Cambridge syllabus. But, while their proportion to the whole varied at each university, both schools taught the same mixture of subjects. Each particular subject was believed to confer its own unique benefit upon the student. The history of his own country was the basis of responsible citizenship and sound general knowledge. The theoretical subjects taught logical reasoning from particular facts to general conclusions, while the special study was intended to provide an introduction to the historian's craft.

Furthermore, there was little difference in the organisation of historical study or the methods employed in teaching it at either university. Instruction was carried on through a combination of lectures, essays and tutorials. Rather more emphasis was laid on the essay at Oxford, where the tutorial system was more deeply ingrained and more formal; but the Conversation Class inspired by Seeley was adopted by other Cambridge lecturers, and all students were ensured some personal supervision, though not always in their own college. Both Schools deployed an inter-collegiate lecture scheme and with similar results. At Cambridge, because of pressure on a small body of teachers, the system was more official and run by the History Board. It made much greater use of the professoriate and for many years the professorial names on the lecture list outnumbered those of the college tutors. Not until Seeley's death could the Regius Professor afford to lecture off the syllabus.

The list of great names emerging from Oxford in the 1870s – often cited as proof of the Oxford School's superior quality – is due in great measure to the lure of the Brackenbury Scholarship at Balliol, which for many years was the only prestigious financial incentive open to those wishing to study history. The emergence of King's and Trinity as centres of historical teaching in Cambridge did much to restore a balance in the 1890s.[8]

Writing in 1884, a year before the reforms which based the Cambridge special subject firmly upon original sources, Paul Fredericq could find little by which to distinguish the two Schools. Their presentation of historical outlines and accompanying theoretical subjects was unrivalled by the Continental universities, and the benefits conferred by the English system of intensive private reading were nothing short of impressive. But in Fredericq's eyes both Schools suffered from the same, single, intrinsic defect. They did not train historical scholars.

At first glance, Fredericq's argument seems somewhat perverse. The study of original authorities had long been a dominant feature of the Oxford History School. Though only an introduction, it was intended to lead the student to consider the importance of original authorities and to learn how history was put together. Indeed, so deeply was this principle ingrained that A. H. Johnson declared that:

> The aim of the School is to furnish at once the basis of a liberal education, and, in the case of those who aim at a high class, to teach the principles upon which the study and criticism of original authorities should be pursued.[9]

The Cambridge reforms of 1885 were prompted by Creighton, Cunningham, Prothero and Gwatkin, on the basis that the Tripos failed to provide an adequate training in the use of original authorities, and therefore that it did not familiarise the future historian with even the rudiments of his craft.

Fredericq was aware of the Oxford special subject. But he denied its effectiveness in securing a thorough historical training. English students, he said, were not 'sufficiently familiar' with the sources of history, and the techniques necessary to a proper analysis of them. He dismissed Seeley's view that it was dangerous to begin research work too early with the retort that:

> as yet no better method of making historians has been discovered . . . until the student has been brought face to face with documents apparently contradictory which he must criticise and account for, he can have no idea of the scientific structure of history. Perhaps some gifted minds can train themselves after leaving the university; but how much time . . . the princes of the science would save them.

Fredericq was convinced that with their powerful and well organised teaching systems the English universities would soon extend their scope to provide further for impending scholars.[10]

What value have the words of a Continental scholar who had evidently failed to grasp the nature of, and the principles underlying, an English liberal education, where, though preparation for a man's after-life was no longer thought distasteful, it was regarded as a benefit incidental to the chief end of mental training? The answer is that Fredericq's views as to the future of English historical teaching were remarkably prophetic. The idea that a university's chief function was to advance research, and that the primary role of a history department was to train scholars to assist in that capacity, was seized upon and developed by a vocal minority of historical scholars who reached academic maturity in the two decades following Fredericq's report.

It had always been assumed that history Schools would make some contribution to the development of the discipline if only through the professoriate, which was expected to carry out, and therefore to stress the importance of, research. The professor's function had been defined by the University Commissions of the 1850s and since confirmed by the labours of Stubbs, Seeley, Burrows, Creighton, Freeman and Froude. The professor was charged with teaching duties, and when he took an active role in departmental administration Seeley established a precedent which others soon adopted. But the professor's supreme duty remained research. He was to establish himself as the chief representative of learning. It was a role which Stubbs assumed with ease, and one to which Seeley self-consciously aspired. Both published learned and stimulating works which helped to establish the Regius Chair at the forefront of historical learning. In future, accredited published work became an essential criterion of a candidate for a professorial post. Freeman and Froude and Bury won their Chairs on the basis of their books. Creighton gained preference over Gwatkin in the election to the Dixie Chair because he had written a 'big book' while Gwatkin had concentrated his energies on teaching for two Triposes.[11] Acton succeeded Seeley, and York Powell Froude, on the grounds of reputation and promise.

Bury, Tout and Firth therefore broke no new ground when they defined their professorial function in terms of advancing the study of history through the prosecution of detailed research. But unlike their distinguished predecessors their declaration of intent was made in a new, forceful and deliberately challenging manner. No longer content to define and fulfil their duties to science outside the established boundaries of the curriculum, they sought to reduce the distinction between the dual functions of teaching and research by teaching research techniques. Firth declared in his inaugural lecture that:

if the study of history means an endeavour to add to this common inheritance of knowledge, surely the teaching of history means an endeavour to train men capable of adding to knowledge? This, at all events is the principle upon which I base my conception of my duty here.[12]

Firth maintained that a training in the techniques of historical research should be a part of the education of every undergraduate reading for the School. The special subject was not an adequate means to this end and the syllabus should therefore be adjusted accordingly. He did not decry the importance of history as a medium of education, but called for a readjustment of the balance between the claims of a liberal education and those of direct vocational training. It was a principle with which professorial colleagues at Cambridge and Manchester concurred, and one which all, with varying degrees of success, took practical measures to implement. Though their antecedents can be traced much earlier, these views were expressed most forcibly between 1903, when J. B. Bury delivered his inaugural lecture at Cambridge, and 1906, when T. F. Tout discussed 'Schools of History' at Newnham College. Firth's long campaign came spectacularly to public notice between the two in 1904. This widespread but chronologically concurrent expression of similar ideas about the ideal nature of a university history school represents a very definite 'movement' in educational thinking on the subject. The 'new movement' to establish a more thorough and complete training as an integral part of an undergraduate's education was underpinned by two complex but interrelated developments.

First, among historians in the late 1860s there was a growing self-consciousness that they had begun to form a profession, set apart from the general body of 'men of letters' by a strict code of practice. It was a code which demanded a thorough, systematic and critical appraisal of original authorities, and which postulated a sober and unspectacular appreciation of its own function. As a rule, no longer were historians to be concerned primarily with entertaining the reading public, with predicting the future course of politics, or with vindicating party prejudice. Their task was to increase man's knowledge of the past. They were to contribute to a stockpile of historical data, what Firth called 'a common inheritance of knowledge'. The historian who toiled in this great scheme of things was, said Bury, engaged ultimately in an 'act of faith'. Though there were

notable dissenting voices, few historical writers sought to undermine this definition of professional history as 'science'. Scientific,
that is, in method and in a dispassionate and objective search for
truth, but not scientific in the sense of establishing universal laws.
Much misunderstood, Bury coined the phrase 'History is a science,
no less, no more', to express the concept of history as a data bank
established and verified by research techniques, and to distinguish it
from the older, more philosophical interpretations of history. How
did this new brand of professional historian emerge?

The question has no easy or simple answer. While plausible
hypotheses have been advanced, a satisfactory solution has yet to be
discovered. The latest attempt suggests that in the 1860s and '70s a
'new-style' history emerged from a mixture of reverence for the
methods of natural science and for the canons of German scholarship, which had begun to flower in the first half of the nineteenth
century. Professor Heyck suggests that the methods employed, and
the possibilities suggested, by the natural sciences caught the imagination of English historians, who, after flirting with and then rejecting
the possibility of 'positivist' history, turned to the vigorous model of
German historical scholarship, which seemed to embody all that
they admired in natural science. Freeman, Green and Stubbs, the
'Oxford school' of historians, are cited as the prime example of this
process. They stressed the scientific nature of historical research and
adopted a healthy robust Germanic insistence on writing history for
its own sake, independent of moral, political or religious aims which
was rapidly assimilated by their colleagues.[13]

This is an interesting and stimulating hypothesis, but one fraught
with problems. The influence of German on English historiography
is a highly contentious question. The more so because it has been
used as a convenient label by which to explain change for so long
that it has become dogma. While many historians claimed to look to
Germany almost as a Platonic form of the historical enterprise,
others roundly denied the extent of Germanic influence and were
proud to assert their own intellectual independence.[14] Recent studies suggest that while many late nineteenth-century American
academics believed that they had adopted a Germanic approach to
historical study they were simply refining and standardising trends
that had long been present before history was 'academicised'

through its incorporation in the formal institutional structure of higher education.[15] A similar trend can be discerned in England. While it is, of course, fallacious to argue that German studies did not exert any influence on English academic life, nevertheless there is strong evidence to suggest that it was at its height in the first half of the century, long before Freeman, Green and Stubbs began serious historical work, and that this influence, such as it was, was transmitted less through the medium of modern than of ancient history, biblical criticism and philosophy. These studies were highly developed and their impact was well established before natural science had made any marked influence upon English intellectual life. The 'ancient' historians employed 'scientific' research techniques before mid-century, and 'modern' historians like Macaulay, Palgrave and Allen made copious use of original authorities.[16] It can be argued that the opening of the archives, the production of the Rolls Series and the reform of the Public Record Office made it easier (and therefore more likely) for most historians to reach and study original documents, a study which since the turn of the century had become something of a trend, and that the advances of German scholarship and its growing support structure were cited not as something unique, but as a milestone against which present British efforts could be measured.

While we may conjecture at length about the influence of Germany on the development of a self-conscious historical profession, what is more certain is that the new wave of historical scholars did not "imitate" the methods of the natural sciences. The point is important because the concept of history as 'science' underlay the campaign by Bury, Firth and Tout for the further extension of a professional training in research techniques. The 'new school', with Tout as its most vocal advocate, all stressed the 'scientific' nature of the historian's task. But rather than as a 'paradigm for the acquisition of knowledge', the concept of science offered an analogy which historians adopted in order to stress the objective and academic nature of the historical enterprise. 'The easiness of history,' said Tout, 'is due to its lying so near our interests, to its expressing itself in our language, to the immense number of facile generalities and facts, which we can read and get up in our arm-chairs from English books'.[17] For the 'new school' the concept of science was not a model upon which to base their activities, but a vehicle of expression by which to drive its seriousness home to others. Most historians denied strenuously that history was, or ever could be, an exact science, and it was this aspect of the study of the natural sciences which held the greatest appeal to a society enticed by the pursuit of certainty.[18] By adopting scientific terminology and then by disclaiming any desire to draw up laws, historians were ringing their own boundary not only between scholarship and popular literature, but also between scholarship and science, and were therefore helping to define the exact nature of their own profession. Historical scholarship was 'scientific' only in the sense that it involved the mastery of a definite objective and severe method and technique.

The second important development which underlay the campaign for an historical training was based on a gradual enlargement of the national conception of the university's role. From mid-century there had been growing concern that the universities were not accepting sufficient responsibility for the advancement of knowledge. The endowed professoriate was simply not capable of doing enough research to keep Britain abreast of other countries in the production of scholarly work. Jowett began the protest which culminated in Appleton's campaign for 'the endowment of research'.[19] It had considerable effect. The University Commission of 1877 did much to encourage research. It gave life to the Common University Fund at Oxford and Cambridge, through which were established new Chairs and readerships and the 'Prize Fellowship', which could be (though for many years rarely was) granted on the basis of research work or research potential. Money was made available for the latest scientific apparatus, provision was made for instruction in extra-curricular studies like palaeography and numismatics, and in the mid-1890s universities were empowered to award degrees on the basis of research – though they made little impact on the schools of history before the Great War.[20]

The campaign for the endowment of research was vociferous, and though it by no means attained 'mass' support it did lead the universities to recognise a formal duty to the advancement of knowledge. But it was an extra-curricular duty. The changes brought about by the Common University Funds had little effect on the history syllabus at Oxford or Cambridge. Though the ancient universities recognised an expansion in the research industry they were by no means geared wholeheartedly to its prosecution. A firm line was still drawn between teaching and research, and the deployment of one function did not always imply that the other would follow as a matter of course. Lord Curzon put it quite plainly in 1908. 'Education is one thing and the spirit of inquiry is another.' The two oldest universities were in no doubt as to which was most important.[21]

The new school of historians who planned their careers around the production of scholarly books took a distinctly different view. Tout declared openly that 'The true measure of academic progress is the share which the university takes in the advancement of knowledge and the part which it plays in training its alumni in original investigation.' To Tout education was a secondary concern. Like him, Bury believed strongly that history schools must begin to 'turn out' in larger numbers 'a new kind of critical antiquarian' capable at once of contributing to the cause of historical truth. Firth agreed.[22] To these historians history was a science which would never develop fully without a primed body of technicians working constantly at it, and it was a science which could not be practised efficiently without a specialist training of the sort currently lacking in Britain. They aimed to remedy the deficiency. But who would they train? Tout claimed that 'even more important than the honour schools is the post-graduate . . . work of a university.' Initially efforts were pitched at the postgraduate level B.Litt., Certificate of Advanced Training and M.A. degrees. But it soon became clear that the avenues for postgraduate students were not proving sufficiently attractive to encourage a large postgraduate class. The reasons were not far to seek. There were few scholarships for postgraduate study, and still fewer jobs for young historians who had completed their training. Oxbridge fellowships were the most common opening for intending historians and Firth lamented, 'I cannot infer from anything I have seen that possession of a proper professional training for the study of history is one of the requisites held necessary for teaching it.' It was not, and for clear reasons. Colleges still held primary responsibility for the education of undergraduates. Lecturers and tutors were elected to teach. That was their appointed function. And despite the claims of the new school there seemed little evidence that a grounding in research would help a tutor to push a man through the Schools with increased efficiency. Was not York Powell dismissed by Trinity College for failing systematically to produce good results? Quite simply, success in the Schools was regarded as the best test of a man's fitness to ensure that success in others.[23]

The 'new school' turned then to the system of undergraduate teaching. In default of an efficient postgraduate network they would incorporate the rudiments of a basic historical training in the syllabus itself. If the special subject was not sufficiently well adapted to this end, it must be altered substantially to reflect it.

This was where the campaign caught light. Most tutors were keen to maintain the distinction between education and research. They held with Curzon that the university was still 'and must remain the great national training ground for those of our youths who aspire to a broad and liberal education.' They maintained that the introduction of a specialist research training into the Honours course was highly inappropriate – indeed, the campaign to establish the Institute of Historical Research grew from a widespread belief that the universities could not, and probably should not, attempt to cater fully for the needs of historical research while fulfilling their essential role as educators of the nation's developing intellect.[24]

Tout, Firth and Bury all believed the distinction between education and research to be a false one, and maintained strongly that teaching research techniques conveyed a unique educational benefit. Nevertheless, while conducted on the same basis, their individual campaigns met with differing measures of success. The differences are attributable to two main things. First, the determination and administrative skills of the individuals involved. Second, and more decisive, the strength of ideas about the value of existing educational practice embodied in long-standing and highly complex institutional structures. The interrelationship is best uncovered by looking more closely at the campaign for change at each university.

'Clashing ideals': Cambridge, 1895–1914

Bury had high ideals. But he instituted no radical measures in the Cambridge syllabus, and exerted little influence upon the practical development of historical studies there. But he inherited Acton's

Chair at a time of peace between the two warring factions, which on Seeley's death had met in 'two pitched battles weekly' for almost two years. At the end even the patient had become restless, and the most aggressive reformer weary of the fight. But there had been agreement among all members of the board that change was necessary, so when a settlement was reached, and one that was agreeable to and catered for the interests of both 'historians' and 'political scientists', the question of reform had exhausted itself. It became a dead letter. The nature of the early reforms is instructive, and, in combination with Bury's somewhat lethargic attitude to administrative chores, helps to explain why, though he shared similar ideals, Bury made little effort to create a history school in the manner of Tout or Firth.

After Seeley's death – so soon in fact that it was almost before Acton (whose influence in this matter has been vastly overstated, and is now a part of the mystique which surrounds his tenure of the Cambridge Chair) had become a recognisable figure at Trinity high table – change was in the air.[25] It was felt generally that the Tripos was badly organised. Subjects were jumbled and mixed and being taken up by students before they were ready to benefit from them. Almost all, college tutors and professors alike, could be persuaded to agree that the Tripos must be divided. The first part, spread over two years, would ensure that the student had what Cunningham called 'a basic grounding' in history, while the second would allow him to indulge his tastes and to specialise – which in Cambridge meant a deeper study of 'history proper', or a wider study of the cognate sciences.[26]

The board's notion of 'a basic grounding' in history is at once interesting and enlightening. It had generally been recognised that the Tripos was deficient in its lack of European history. After much discussion it was agreed that, while ancient history should become an optional subject, all students must have a basic knowledge of the outlines of European history, and that this would be combined with a deeper knowledge of English history and an acquaintance with political science. But the battles of 1885 had not been forgotten. 'A basic grounding' in history included the Special Historical Subject, which was made compulsory on all students in Part I, but, in the conciliatory nature of reform, not in Part II. Every student must, as a basic requirement, have a knowledge of historical outlines and how to use original authorities.[27]

The second part of the Tripos bore the fruits of compromise between the tradition which Seeley established and the wishes of the 'historians'. With a basic knowledge of history secured, both in outline and in method, the candidate was at liberty to devote himself to historical or theoretical studies and to cut his own pathway through the mountain range of options which awaited him. The preamble to the board's final draft report spelled out that the new Tripos would 'maintain the best traditions of the Historical school, and afford a sufficient choice of subjects to the various classes of students whom it is desirable to attract to an history Tripos'. Both parties to the reform realised this fact. While Maitland 'confessed that on one or two points he had been overruled rather than convinced by Dr. Sidgwick, Professor Marshall and Mr. Browning', and that he 'thought the programme was much too English, much too unhistorical and much too miscellaneous', that 'it resembled rather the programme of a variety show than the sober programme of an Historical school', he was aware that in the absence of an economic or political science Tripos the history school had to cater for two types of student, those for whom Seeley had begun his conversation class, and those for whom Prothero and Creighton had helped establish the special subject. While few of the board members expressed themselves completely satisfied with the scheme, Leathes was not alone when he said that its merits hinged on the fact that it 'made concessions based on mutual compromise, both to students of political science, and to students of history'.[28]

The practical results of this compromise are interesting. They show how two men as far apart as Gwatkin and Marshall could express themselves content with the scheme. In Part II, which occupied his last year, the student read English constitutional history, and then completed his basic grounding by rounding off the outline course in European history. He then had a choice. He could sit a minimum of two or a maximum of four other papers. If he so desired he could spend the greater part of his final year reading for one or two special subjects. Even the most fanatical advocate of an historical training could not deny that, theoretically at least, the student's last year formed a good bridge between the Tripos and historical research. Henry Gwatkin was a firm believer in the educational value of teaching research techniques. He aimed to introduce his own students to original authorities, and to:

> rouse interest, to give the guiding facts, and to teach the principles of research and criticism which enable men not only to become their own teachers, but to return and see for themselves how far we rightly gave them the guiding facts.

Gwatkin was keen to maintain the balance between historical fact and historical method – between a liberal education and an historical training – and he was sure that,

> In Cambridge . . . the Historical Tripos will now give an excellent training in historical method. A man who goes through . . . and takes a good place in his Second Part, has laid a broad foundation for future work.[29]

The conscious adjustment which the board made between the claims of two local factions, combined with the important innovation of dividing the Tripos (thereby marking a distinction between preliminary study – which included an introduction to historical sources – and special study) made it difficult to want for more. A close reading of Bury's inaugural lecture suggests that he was aware of this fact. Trevelyan's hysterical reaction to Bury's statement of history as science has tended to obscure the heart of Bury's argument.

Bury expressed a strong belief in the importance of research and the importance of training research workers. But he held back any criticisms of the Cambridge curriculum, which, given the restrictive nature of the examination system, seemed to make sensible provision for such study. Firth's inaugural lecture caused anger in Oxford, not because of his views on research, which were no more radical than those of Bury, but because he openly condemned the system run by his fellow tutors. Tout's efforts at Manchester gained much publicity, but then Tout was charged with recreating the system through which he put his views into being. Bury, however, accepted the importance of the institutional structure through which history must be taught. Restrictive as the examination system was, it made generous provision for the development of research skills at a time

in the student's course when he was able to appreciate the continuity of history which Bury, like Tout, regarded as an essential
feature of any historical education. So, while Bury made his own
views about history perfectly clear, he was able to avoid direct
controversy with the History Board.

Nevertheless, while the framework was sound enough, in that the
student was allowed to specialise in his final year, Bury, like Firth,
began to doubt the efficacy of the special subject as the means by
which to train students in historical method. Bury was concerned
that the special subject was not achieving what in theory it was
intended to achieve, and in 1907 made his only serious effort to
change the system.[30]

The special subject, he said, was 'intended to secure that history
Honours students shall acquire some general acquaintance with the
processes by which history is derived from sources'. Candidates
were to learn to appreciate historical method. The subject of the
special study was not as important as the techniques which working
at it should confer. The student should not be expected to make the
facts relating to the special subject part of his 'mental furniture', as he
would the facts relating to general European or to English history.
Their object was different. But this, said Bury, was where the special
subject failed. It was testing the wrong kind of ability. There were too
many questions demanding strict factual information. The student
had to learn the historical facts of the period in question in order to
describe scenes or incidents relating to his subject. This was an effort
of memory, not a test of technique. The real object was to find out
whether he could compare sources and evaluate evidence, but the
student found that he was expected to be able to identify the context
of an isolated passage in one authority, and then to compare it with
what he could remember from passages in other authorities concerning the same point. The act of memory involved in such a task,
said Bury, defeated the purpose of the special subject. It got in the
way of training, and meant that the student was 'required to do
things which have no relation to the practical business of historical
investigation and the criticism of sources'. Anyone who wrote
history had his sources in front of him. The crucial test was his ability
to use them critically. The special subject failed to simulate such
conditions, and therefore the history school was failing in part of its

task.

Bury doubted if the traditional method of examination used not only at Cambridge, but also at Oxford and Manchester, was a suitable means of testing whether the requisite skills had been acquired. Like Firth and Tout he maintained that 'the ideal test in the use of authorities is a dissertation'. But he was also pragmatic. He was aware of the grip which examinations exercised over the university system. He did not pursue the point which Prothero had taken up and lost twenty years earlier. Instead he sought to modify the examination itself, by adopting the needs of an historical training to it as closely as was possible. What was required, said Bury, was an open book examination, and a different type of question.

Questions of source characterisation, questions of interpretation, and questions involving the reconstruction of incidents would be retained, while the factual details surrounding the period would be omitted. Authorities would be available for consultation during the examination, which, said Bury, would give greater scope to the candidate's historical ability while at the same time defeating that pernicious element – the 'surcharged' memory.

Bury had made his point. 'Thus amended,' he said, 'the Tripos would probably secure as good an education in history as can reasonably be expected under the examination system.' But his attempts to improve historical training and to make the Tripos a better basis for research failed. A committee headed by J. R. Tanner and H. M. Gwatkin – both enthusiastic advocates of research – dismissed his proposal to implement an open book examination. They concluded that the burden on the memory was an unfortunate but sadly unavoidable by-product of any mode of historical study. They also believed that the candidate should possess a more general knowledge of the period in which his special subject was set. They took the view that it was important that the candidate understood events in a wider context. Opinion was that the special subject was a good test of historical ability.[31] As Bury complained to Tout, 'the idea prevails that they are the cream of the papers'. The implementation of an open book examination paper was too grave a break with a well established, comfortably administered system to be entertained with any seriousness.[32]

Indeed, the Cambridge Tripos remained largely unaltered until the Great War. Though the new Economics Tripos, founded in 1903, meant that theoretically less provision was necessary for the cognate sciences, the balance between the Seeleyan tradition and the pure history Tripos – what J. S. Reid called 'clashing ideals' – was maintained, and its preservation outranked all other considerations.

'It requires more than one person to make a system': Oxford, 1895–1914

Reform at Oxford was debated by the general body of tutors in 1898. As at Cambridge three years earlier, there was a general feeling that the machinery of examination could profitably be overhauled. But, unlike Cambridge, there were few compromises to be had. Oxford was pleased with its History School. Fine points of detail were all that were questioned.

The Board of Modern History and the association were almost unanimously behind the idea of the university as primarily an educational institution. Their conception of the History School dovetailed neatly with this belief. Through the thorough study of history, students would receive an exacting mental training. In educational terms the distinction between modern history and classics was one of means, not ends. Despite growls from York Powell, the exiled prince of knowledge, the idea of training students for research did not make its mark in 1898.

Powell was one of the first university-based teachers to suggest that the university-based schools of history should aim to train scholars. He was, said F. M. Powicke, 'the most stimulating and disturbing factor in this movement'.[33] Stimulating because of his charismatic air, disturbing because he lacked verve, drive and self-discipline. Powell's influence on the development of historical studies at Oxford was minimal. Having ranged his acute knowledge of his own shortcomings against the enormous strength of the tutorial body, the new Regius Professor chose to maintain a low profile. While his views on the nature of history and an historical education spread quickly through correspondence and word of mouth, Powell had little of the missionary zeal which possessed Firth and Tout. He was asked to teach at Liverpool. There, with effort, he might conceivably have done for Liverpool what Tout did for Manchester. But the offer was refused. 'I think,' he concluded, 'I can do more good in Oxford in small ways.' Like Acton, he made his mark on individuals, and, like Acton, he influenced the future direction of many fine historical scholars. Maitland's summary is apposite. 'York Powell was one of those men whom it did one good to meet.'

But Powell's lack-lustre approach to his official duties upset, disturbed and invariably saddened some of his colleagues. 'The business of a Professor,' said George Porthero, 'is to teach; to organise . . . study and learning; [and] to advance the limits of human knowledge by research.' Powell despised teaching and examining. 'I have all sorts of faults,' he said to J. M. Mackay. 'I am almost as casual as you are, I hate the idea of exam passing. I don't care for stupid folks who ought to be clerks to manure-carts instead of wearing black clothes and sitting at desks scribbling out commercial damnation. . . .'[34]

Perhaps Powell could have said and done much to encourage the prosecution of research at Oxford. But writing did not come easily to him, and as an organiser he was congenitally incapable. His inaugural lecture, for which he was late, lasted only twenty minutes. Despite strong views on the composition of the History School, which he described as 'pure humbug . . . not history but memorising', this was his last attempt to state or to lead radical opinion in Oxford. Like Stubbs, he had not the heart to wage a long campaign for change.[35]

Powell's only effort to encourage the provision for research was embodied in a committee report on the needs of the School. The board called for money for a seminar; 'roughly defined as an historical laboratory in which a small class of advanced students co-operate at working at a definite historical subject, using always original authorities, and directed and assisted by a teacher', who, of course, was Powell. The principle was interesting. The board was recognising research and instruction in research techniques. But only when it was taught 'after school', as an extra-curricular activity. The distinction between historical training and historical education was maintained clearly.[36] Powell was not geared to influence the cause of reform. He made no mark on the curriculum because he made no effort to do so. Not so Charles Firth.

The discussion of reform in 1898 hinged on efforts to reduce the strain on the candidate's memory. There were few proposals of a radical nature. Even the Cambridge experiment of dividing the course was dismissed as overly innovative. A. L. Smith summed up the general mood when he said that the board must have a care to 'avoid even the appearance of pulling up the plant by the roots to see if it is growing'. Though the machinery was tinkered with, the vehicle of education remained substantially unchanged.

Firth watched the proceedings with dismay. In the absence of words from Powell, by whom he was much influenced, he felt it his duty to speak out with characteristic bluntness. 'At present,' he claimed:

> the weak point of the School is that it produces journalists, politicians, and well-informed men, but does not train historians. It does not give even the first class man a training which fits him to do decent historical work. . . . We turn him out unable to read historical documents, unless they are very modern ones, unaccustomed to the use of original authorities, and unacquainted with historical bibliography. In short, he has none of the technical knowledge or training an historian ought to have, and has to pick it up for himself. We ought to do something to alter this state of things in our proposed changes.[37]

Firth, like Bury, obviously did not find the special subject an adequate avenue to a thorough historical training. It had not helped him. But, like Bury, he was studiously ignored. What he believed to be 'the weak point of the School' could be and was dismissed as irrelevant in an institution which had pledged itself to turning out 'well informed men'. In 1898 Firth had no support. But his outburst was no surprise to his colleagues.

Firth had been a constant agitator for change. But he was a man apart. Early in his career he abandoned the idea of teaching and threw his energies into research, which became an all-absorbing passion. He soon realised the deficiencies of his own training in preparing him for the career which, as a man of means with few financial worries he had elected to pursue. Partly from views borrowed from Powell, and partly from reflections on the shortcomings of his Oxford education, he assembled his own bandwagon and from it proclaimed that historical research was a scientific procedure which could and should be taught and learned by students of the subject. Firth had strong views and an unabashed confidence in their merit which, combined with a roguish enthusiasm for the rough and tumble of academic debate, brought him constantly to the forefront of board meetings. He was convinced that time would bring reason in its wake. He wrote to Tout, then an ex-officio member of the board, in 1892. 'I think this is a case,' he said:

> in which we are so indubitably right, that we ought to stick to our guns and fight it out. At present no doubt we shall be defeated. The opinions of Smith and Johnson will probably carry the day. ... In a few years however, you and I (if we can get our great works published) will have more reputation and more power than they have. Let us state our programme clearly now and educate our colleagues up to it.[38]

Firth summed up those views in 1898. They seemed to run against the grain of the Oxford system, to be ranged diametrically against long-standing views 'on questions of educational principle and practice'. When Firth was appointed to the Regius Chair the School prepared itself for the shock waves. H. W. C. Davis wrote to Tout:

> Come by all means for Wednesday night. It is only fitting that you should support Firth at his Inaugural. You will have the pleasure of hearing him castigate the Oxford tutorial system.[39]

Davis was quite right. Firth used the occasion to give vent to his accumulative frustration. The furore caused by his lecture was more the result of his intemperate statements about the Oxford system than about his specific proposals for the provision of a research training. But Firth's accusations, directed as they were against the tutorial body, are important. They reveal that as professor he believed the Oxford History School to be split into two distinct groups: the tutorial and the professorial. Furthermore, the tutors' unprecedented display of self-consciousness in their own defence is the one and only clear statement of principle emanating from the silent majority who formed the core of the teaching profession.

Important to an understanding of Firth's lecture is the separation of the concrete from the contentious, of the sound proposals from the provocative and divisive statements. First and foremost he called for a reconsideration of the ends of an historical education. In his eyes the Oxford History School had 'one great defect': it did not train men capable of adding to knowledge. This he believed to be an important aspect of any educational course. But he admitted that many – indeed, perhaps the majority – felt that the true function of an History School was to provide students with a general education which would train the mind; that learning history was an instrument of education rather than an end in itself. In accordance with these ideas the present School had no claims to the efficient training of scholars, though it did provide a foundation for such training. In its absence, he maintained, 'the B.Litt. could provide the constitutional foundation upon which any scheme for higher historical education can be based'. He made it clear that as Regius Professor his 'proper function' lay with this 'higher historical education', and that his teaching plan rested upon:

> the principle of leaving to the tutors the education of the men reading for the school, and reserving for the professors and University teachers, with any help they can get from the tutors, the training of those who wish to carry their studies further.[40]

These would be the 'best men' and postgraduate students.

There was little that could be construed as contentious in these proposals. Like Stubbs, like Freeman, like Froude and York Powell, Firth was simply claiming the age-old professorial right of training 'the best men' outside 'school hours'. He was expressing a division of function between college teacher and university professor. His only proposal for the modification of the curriculum in favour of research was that submissions for prize essays ought to be taken into account by examiners when judging the special subject. Like Bury, Firth believed that working with the sources was a better test of historical ability than a heavy reliance on memory. This was hardly an outrageous proposal.

But Firth mixed his concrete plans in fire and brimstone. He claimed that, while the School aimed at providing a liberal education, its curriculum was inadequate. The examination system simply ensured that the School provided 'an excellent training for journalists'. He made it clear that he believed that the tutors did not and could not lay claim to any influence over future historical work, so denying them any satisfaction they might have in their ex-pupils' successes, and reducing their status to that of the old-fashioned coach. Most cutting of all, however, Firth implied that the existence of a tutorial body undermined the importance of the B.Litt. degree, and would prevent him from exercising any influence over the future direction of historical studies. Firth claimed that the system maintained by the tutors would prevent undergraduates from visiting the professor. They would not have the leisure from their routine work. The professor would have to deal solely with graduates. But what incentive was the B.Litt. degree, when fellowships did not require evidence of research skills? 'After a man's place in the class list,' claimed Firth, 'the social gift called "getting on with the men" is the qualification that counts most.' His lecture was a cry of frustration. He had defined his own function but his hands were tied. He would not be allowed to carry it out. His plans were almost certain to fail. And 'the chief impediment' would be 'the system of historical education which the other teachers of . . . [the] subject had organised'. He was the victim of a tutorial conspiracy.[41]

The tutorial reply – signed by some twenty-three tutors, including Hodgkin, Firth's son-in-law, and Poole and Davis, who were in favour of some research training – reveals just how deeply Firth's comments had cut. Three principles are clearly in evidence. Firstly, that the School was part of the Faculty of Arts, 'and aims at the ideals of a humane and liberal education through the medium of history and the other allied subjects, for which the university as a place of education exists'. Most candidates expected a liberal education, and, while the tutors sympathised with Firth's concern for 'the best men', they did not believe that their cause could be advanced by undermining the system which provided adequately for the majority.

Secondly, they did not wish to adjust the present balance between education and training. They believed the School already provided a good introduction to historical study. They maintained that both constitutional history and the special subject were based on the study of authorities, and as such afforded 'both teachers and pupils invaluable opportunities for laying the basis of some of the qualifications emphasised' by Firth. A long list of graduates of the School now involved in teaching and writing history – which included that of the Regius Professor himself – was cited as positive proof of the School's success in providing a foundation for future work.

Thirdly, the tutors asserted that teaching was a skilled profession in its own right. An underlying sympathy for the plight of the lesser man, which Firth had denigrated, was but one facet of a skill which was essential if the university was to maintain its primary function as a place of education.[42]

Many – indeed, almost all – of the commentators on this debate have cited the pamphlet as a firm punch on the nose for an outspoken and errant professor.[43] But they have been swayed by rhetoric. In the pamphlet the tutors stated their position and defended the importance of their function as teachers in relation to the wishes of the majority of undergraduates. But they did make concessions to the research ideal. They pledged support publicly for the B.Litt. programme. They suggested that colleges could begin to encourage research. And they agreed in principle to the institution of a thesis and the assessment of prize essays. In his heart Firth, like Tout, was calling for a recognition of a readjustment of the primary function of the university. But he was pragmatic enough to ask simply for recognition of research training in the ordinary syllabus of the School. Without conceding any ground on the principle of ultimate ends, the tutors were prepared to go half-way to meet Firth and to accommodate his plans.[44]

On 17 June the tenure of the lectureships in palaeography and diplomatic was extended. On 20 October 1905 essays submitted for the Stanhope, Lothian and Cobden prizes were allowed for assessment in the Final examination. Firth went ahead, with full support from the board, with his programme of Advanced Historical Training which though hampered by a general lack of funds – the bane of all extra-curricular schemes – was broad-ranging and extensive.[45]

Nevertheless the courses were not well attended. As Firth had predicted, the pressures imposed by the Schools dictated that only graduates could find sufficient time to attend the classes. Between 1897 and 1914 only thirty-six candidates read for the B.Litt. degree in history. Only eight were from Oxford. Firth was not training the best men. In recognition of this fact he concentrated his energies on the curriculum. If he could not use the B.Litt. as an introductory course in research skills an equivalent test must be made available to those reading for the B.A.

In 1906, with support from Vinogradoff, he proposed that a thesis be made a part of study for the special subject. Like Bury, he defended the idea on the grounds that the special subject should be a test of method and not of memory. Like the historian, the candidate should be allowed to display his talents with the authorities at hand. Firth supported his proposal by making the suggestion – adopted also by Tout – that:

> the inclusion of a thesis in the course for the B.A. degree will benefit both classes of candidates taking the School, that is, both those who take it for purposes of general education, and those who take it as a special preparation for the study of history.

In the hope that it might cut across the barrier between education and research, Firth was stressing that the mental effort involved in comparing the sifting sources was a valuable educational exercise in its own right, independent of specialist concerns.[46]

Though his proposal was attacked on the grounds that it was not possible to examine or to judge a thesis in relation to other examination papers, and that it would 'tempt undergraduates ... to run before they can walk,' for once he had the tide of opinion flowing with him. The examiners' report of 1905 had warned that much of the information appearing in answers to special subject papers was not coming from original authorities. The lecture system was defeating the true ends of the special subject. In 1906 the examiners again pointed out that the specials were poorly done. Even men who had taken First Class degrees had scored B grades in their special subject. The balance between a general education and an historical training, even an elementary historical training, had tipped visibly too far in the direction of the former.[47]

In 1906 a faculty committee suggested that a thesis be considered as an alternative to the special subject. In real terms the concession was not dramatic. The thesis represented only one paper. It was only a small part of a large examination. But Firth had won a point. Training in the techniques of research was recognised as an integral part of the School's programme, and one in which it was important to maintain a high standard of attainment. It had been conceded that the special subject did not always meet those requirements.

In March 1907 provision for submission of theses was included in the syllabus of the School.[48] But it was not made compulsory, as Firth had hoped. Students could elect to write a thesis in lieu of one special subject paper. Results were mixed. Between 1909 and 1914 only twenty-five candidates submitted theses. Standards varied. Only half gained First Class Honours overall. The examiners had mixed feelings. Their reports are instructive. Candidates tended to tackle subjects which were too broad to encompass thoroughly within a year, with the result that many produced sub-standard work, or tended to 'neglect some of the main subjects presented by the School'. Here was a problem which Firth had not anticipated. Students writing theses were not receiving the close supervision required to train them in research techniques. The School was large, and tutors were busy with large classes. The man who tackled a thesis was left on his own. He still had to train himself in the methods of historical investigation, but under severe pressure and with his Class at stake.[49]

Firth had conducted a one-man campaign for research training, and had partially succeeded. But he failed where Tout won conspicuous success. He could not make that training compulsory, or systematic. 'You say that perhaps by this time, I have got a system organised,' he wrote sadly to Tout. 'Unluckily it requires more than one person to make a system.'[50] Firth had ranged his principles and professorial powers against the weight of tradition. The university was primarily a seat of education. The bulk of its institutional structure – colleges, faculties and syllabuses – were geared to an examination system by which the quality of a student's education in terms of the knowledge and skills he had gained was judged. The function of the college teacher was determined by, and his livelihood rested on, the continual pursuit of this end. The college teachers were aware of the fact and defended their role accordingly. Firth had tried to cut across this structure, and with partial success. But it was not in the interests of the larger body to allow him to redefine the ideal nature of an undergraduate's education. The power of tradition and the weight of the system which it underpinned held him back.

NOTES TO CHAPTER 7

1   G. W. Prothero, *Why should we learn History? An Inaugural Lecture delivered at Edinburgh*, 16th October 1894 (Edinburgh, 1894), p. 4. See also Prothero, pp. 18–22; Richard Lodge, *The Study of History in a Scottish University: an Inaugural Lecture delivered on October 22 1894* (Glasgow, 1894), pp. 6–7.

2   *Report of the Royal Commission appointed to Inquire into the Depression of Trade and Industry*, 1886 (XXI–XII).

3   Alfred Marshall, A Plea for the Creation of a Curriculum in Economics (Cambridge, 1902). Peter Slee, 'Concern for Skills', Universities quarterly, vol. 40, II, 163–70.

4   See Prothero, Why should we learn History?, pp. 22–3; Lodge, The Study of History, p. 7; C. W. C. Oman, An Inaugural Lecture on the Study of History, February 7 1906 (Cambridge, 1902).

5   For a definition of 'middle class' see F. Musgrove, 'Middle-class education and employment in the nineteenth century', Economic History Review, XII, 1959–60, 99–111. For the expanding middle class professions see H. Perkin, 'Middle-class education and employment in the nineteenth century: a critical note', Economic History Review, XIV, 1961–62, 122–30.

6   I am grateful to Mark Curthoys of the History of Oxford University Project for supplying me with the group's as yet unpublished data on the careers and occupations of Oxford history graduates. Deborah Wormell, Sir John Seeley, p. 119. H. Jenkins and D. Caradog Jones, 'Social data of Cambridge alumni', British Journal of Sociology, vol. 1, 1950, 93–116.

7   For a Cambridge man's view see The Letters of F. W. Maitland, ed. C. H. S. Fifoot (Cambridge, 1965), p. 130, fol. 150. p. 261. fol. 332. For a dissenting view see O. Browning, The Proposed New Tripos (London, 1896), p. 41. For an Oxford man's view see C.U.L. Add. 8119/1/P, 129, R. L. Poole to Lord Acton, 19 February 1895. For dissenting voices see T. F. Tout, Schools of History, p. 10; L. L. Price, The Present Position of Economic Study in Oxford (Oxford, 1902), p. 3.

8   Balliol was Oxford's chief history college. Between 1893 and 1903 it accounted for just over 10% of all Oxford history candidates (only New College took more). For full details see C. H. Firth, Honours in History: Observations on the standard of the Modern History School, 1893–1903 (Oxford, 1983). The list of Brackenbury Scholars includes T. F. Tout (1874), R. Lodge (1875), C. H. Firth (1876), H. W. C. Davis (1891) and J. R. L. Muir (1893). Other Balliol graduates include J. H. Round (1875), R. L. Poole (1878), S. Lee (1882), A. G. Little (1886) and J. Tait (1887). At Cambridge between 1875 and 1895 403 men took Honours in history (102 women took the exams but were not eligible for the degree), 148 were from Trinity and fifty-six from Kings. Trinity took eleven Firsts, fifty-nine Seconds, seventy-eight Thirds, King's nineteen Firsts, twenty-seven Seconds and ten Thirds.

9   Fredericq, The Study of History, pp. 53–4. A. H. Johnson, Faculty of Arts. Honour School of Modern History (Oxford, 1900) p. 1.

10   Fredericq, The Study of History, p. 51, p. 54.

11   Slee, 'H. M. Gwatkin', p. 280.

12   Firth, A Plea for the Historical Teaching of History: an Inaugural Lecture delivered on November 9th 1904 (Oxford, 1904), p. 11.

13   Heyck, The Transformation of Intellectual Life, pp. 139, p. 145.

14   For those who looked to Germany see J. B. Bury, An Inaugural Lecture: delivered in the Divinity School, Cambridge on January 26, 1903 (Cambridge, 1903), pp. 10–19; A. W. Ward, Suggestions towards the Establishment of an Historical Tripos, p. 9; Lord Acton, 'German schools of history', E.H.R., 1 January 1886, pp. 7–42. For dissenting voices see Oman, On the Writing of History, p. viii; An Inaugural Lecture, pp. 24–5; W. A. Shaw, in Selected Essays and Papers of Richard Copley Christie (London, 1902), pp. xix–xx; H. A. L. Fisher, An Unfinished Autobiography (London, 1946), p. 58. For modern assumptions see Olive Anderson, 'The political uses of history', p. 88. For dissenting voices see L. Woodward, 'The rise of the professorial historian in England', in Studies in International History: Essays presented to W. H. Medlicott, ed. K. Bourne and D. C. Watt (London, 1967), pp. 16–34; F. Gilbert, 'European and American historiography', p. 336.

15   Higham, 'The historical profession', p. 11, p. 19.

16   See P. B. M. Blaas, Continuity and Anachronism, who sees the changing historiographical trends of the late nineteenth century as a conscious reaction to literary and Whig history. For English writers and authorities see p. 76. J. Burrow, A Liberal Descent, warns against blanket labels which obscure more than they reveal.

17   Tout, Schools of History, p. 17.

18   Prothero, Why should we learn History?, p. 6. Oman, An Inaugural Lecture, p. 8. For historians and their rejection of science – and society's ambivalence to scientists – see H. Stuart Hughes, Consciousness and Society: the reorientation of European Social Thought, 1890–1930 (London, 1958), ch. 6.

19   Heyck, Transformation of Intellectual Life, pp. 175–87. Lord Curzon, Principles and Methods of University Reform, being a Letter addressed to the University of Oxford (1909), ch. ix, pp. 179–87.

20   The B.Litt. was instituted at Oxford in June 1895. A Certificate of Research was awarded at Cambridge from June 1895 on the basis of original work completed after six terms. Completion allowed the student the B.A. degree. Between 1896 and 1912 only six history students proceeded to the Bachelor's degree in this way, compared with twenty-four in Oxford who took the B.Litt. in history.

21   Curzon, Principles and Methods, p. 180.

22   Tout, 'Four years of development', in Collected Papers, I, pp. 53–59 (p. 54). Bury, An Inaugural Lecture, p. 38. Firth, A Plea, p. 3.

23   Firth, A Plea, p. 28. Tout 'Four years of Development', p. 54. 'An historical laboratory', p. 83. Oliver Elton, Frederick York Powell: a Life (Oxford, 1906), vol. 1, p. 27.

24   For the origins of the I.H.R. see F. Y. Powell, 'The Ecole des Chartes and English records', T.R.H.S., XI, 1897, pp. 31–40 (p. 37); A. Ward, 'Presidential address', T.R.H.S., XIV, 1900, pp. 1–18 (p. 13). G. W. Prothero, 'Presidential address', T.R.H.S., XVI, 1902, vii–xxv (p. xix). A circular was sent out by Ward, on 18 January asking for opinions on a scheme for an I.H.R. A committee of 104 was formed and in 1903 enough money was raised to appoint two lecturers at the London School of Economics. R.H.S., Prothero, PP2/111/4.

25   Slee, History as a Discipline, pp. 426–8.

26   Seeley Library, Minutes of the Special Board, II, 1893–1927, Min. 5 March 1895, Min. 7 May, Min. 18 October, 22 October.

27   Seeley Library, Minutes, II, seventeen meetings, six reports, seven flysheets required before agreement on 9 February 1897, two years after the first discussions.

28   Reporter, XXVII, No. 23, 9 February 1897, pp. 505–11 (pp. 506, 509).

29   H. M. Gwatkin, 'The teaching of ecclesiastical history, in Essays on the Teaching of History, ed. by W. A. J. Archbold (Cambridge, 1901), pp. 1–10 (p. 2, p. 9).

30   Seeley Library, Minutes, II, Min. April 1907, J. B. Bury, 'Memorandum on the Conduct of the Examination in the Special Subjects of the Historical Tripos'.

31   Seeley Library, Minutes, II, Min. May 12 1908, Report of Committee.

32   John Rylands University Library of Manchester, Papers of T. F. Tout, 1/153/4, J. B. Bury to T. F. Tout, 3 February 1906.

33   F. M. Powicke, Historical Study in Oxford: an Inaugural Lecture delivered before the University of Oxford, Feb. 8 1929 (Oxford, 1929), 1.

34   Elton, Frederick York Powell, vol. 1, p. 119, p. 120. The Letters of F. W. Maitland, p. 305. G. W. Prothero, 'F. Y. Powell', Monthly Review, 26, 1907, 85–94 (pp. 86–87). H. A. L. Fisher, An Unfinished Autobiography, pp. 57–9.

35   Oman, On the Writing of History, pp. 242–6. Elton, F. Y. Powell, I, p. 189, p. 357.

36   Bodleian Library, O.U.A., MH/RI/1, Board of Faculty of Arts (Modern History), Reports 27 January 1899–8 June 1912. (20 February 1902, p. 16), MH/M/1/2, 14 June 1902.

37   Bodleian Library, O.U.A. MH/M/1/2, Board of Faculty of Arts (M.H.), Minutes, II, October 1892–February 1910. Minutes, 12 March 1898 – 28 January 1899. 'Opinions from persons engaged in teaching Modern History as to possible reforms in the Final Honours School', p. 5, Appendix 2, attached to Min. 12 March. Firth was supported by Powell's biography, written as the contribution to reform Powell never made. See Elton, pp. 16–17.

38   John Rylands University Library of Manchester, Tout, 1/367/21 Firth to Tout. 13 March 1892.

39 John Rylands University Libary of Manchester, Tout, 1/264/2 Davis to Tout, 4 November 1904.

40 Firth, _A Plea_, p. 26.

41 John Rylands University Library of Manchester, Tout, 1/1143/5/W. H. Stevenson to Tout, December 4 1908, 'I do not think he [Powicke] would be able to get on with the Undergraduates from his political, religious and other views added to his unimpressive physique.' Firth, _A Plea_, pp. 27–30 (p. 30). See also Balliol College, MS Collection, A. L. Smith, Firth to R. M. Hodgkin, 14 November 1904, 'if you think there was anything in what I said . . . which could . . . hurt your feelings, be good enough to let me know'.

42 All Souls College, Codrington Library, G2.6.32.2, To C. H. Firth, M.A.

43 Oman, _On the Writing of History_, p. 246. Marriott, _Memories of Four Score Years_, p. 61. Marriot was not fond of the professors, nor prone to praise them. It was he who said of Stubbs, 'to assess his greatness as an historian would demand a paragraph'.

44 All Souls College, G2.6.32.2.

45 Bodleian Library, GA Oxon. b. 138 (82–85).

46 Bodleian Library, O.U.A. MH/M1/2, II, Min. 10 May 1906, 17 May 1907, 29 November 1907, 4 February 1908. O.U.A. MH/R1/1, p. 50, p. 54.

47 Bodleian Library, O.U.A. MH/R1/1, p. 38, p. 46. UR/L./38/3, Modern History Examiners' notebook, I, 1900–37.

48 _Gazette_, XXVIII, No. 121g, 12 November 1907, p. 145.

49 Bodleian Library, O.U.A. MH/R1/1, Reports, vol. 1, p. 84, 1908 – four theses, (three Firsts); p. 106, 1910 – six theses (two Firsts); p. 150, 1911 – four theses (two Firsts). MH/R1/2, Reports, vol. 2; 1912 – one thesis (one First); 1913 – five theses (two Firsts); 1914 – five theses (two Firsts).

50 John Rylands University Library of Manchester, Tout, 1/367/74, Firth to Tout, 20 June 1905.

CHAPTER 8

'Freedom, a *sine qua non* for success'
TOUT AND MANCHESTER, 1890–1914

At Manchester Thomas Tout won recognition for the principle that a university history school should train its students to do historical research. As a means towards securing this end he implemented the thesis as a compulsory part of the Manchester history degree. His ideas and proposals differed little from those of Bury and Firth. Yet he succeeded completely where they secured only partial gains. Why should this have been so? The answer is disarmingly simple. Tout was the right man in the right place at the right time.

Contemporaries respected Tout's personal qualities. They were considerable. Unlike Bury, Tout enjoyed the hurly-burly of academic rough and tumble. Unlike Firth, he chose his public words carefully. As an administrator he was second to none. Dynamism and a thorough grasp of the issues powered him to the heart of every debate. Though they might not always agree, people always listened.

Tout was also more fortunate than his professorial colleagues-in-arms at Oxford and Cambridge. Through crucial environmental advantages never accorded to Bury or to Firth Tout was able to give free reign to his energy, tact and idealism. Like them, he inherited a healthy, well respected history school which balanced a general knowledge of the facts of British and European history with a rudimentary training in historical method. But, while based on firm foundations, the school was small. In 1890 Tout had two colleagues and on average between three and four Honours students a year. The advantages for anyone considering implementing a programme of reform are obvious. First, consensus was reached more easily among Manchester's three history teachers than among Oxford's thirty. Tout had been appointed to the Chair of history at Owens College to fill the gap left by A. W. Ward's appointment as Principal. Though Ward continued to teach history, each year slowly and deliberately he shed an increasing proportion of his administrative duties, until in 1895 he passed over the departmental headship to Tout. Tout did not as yet have a free hand. The school was still developing its reputation and it was tied to an administrative structure of which University College Liverpool and the Yorkshire College were a weaker and more dependent part. Ward advised Tout to proceed with due caution. When in 1892, following pressure from Firth, Tout had approached the Principal with a view to making the special subject a more practical test of historical ability, Ward responded sympathetically. But he warned Tout that they:

> must be careful to reform slowly, as our students need encouraging rather than frightening. It would be a great pity were the notion to spread that our work is too stiff.[1]

Tout took Ward's advice seriously. As departmental head he made no immediate effort to introduce radical statutory changes to the syllabus. But that did not stop him from experimenting within its confines. This is where the second great advantage of having a small department came into play. With an average of less than four students a year Tout and his colleague James Tait were able to exert a strong personal influence over their charges.

Special subject groups gathered in the Freeman Library. Directed to a subject of which their teacher had specialist knowledge, they worked among the printed sources. Every student was expected to specialise in one particular aspect of the subject and encouraged to write a report about it. It was hard work. Powicke called it 'a hothouse method'. It did not suit everybody. Some gave up under the strain. It certainly would not have worked at Oxford and Cambridge, where classes were too large for such close and sustained personal direction. But at Manchester it produced some impressive results. Of the forty-three students who graduated from Owens

College in History 18 published historical work. The best examples are displayed in a fat volume of essays written by staff and graduates of the school, published in 1902 and intended as a contribution to the campaign for an independent University of Manchester. In the preface Tout and Tait agreed that the requirement for historians to undertake research work among primary sources was well and clearly understood. But they stated emphatically that 'in England the effective encouragement of such research is still almost entirely left to the individual'. They pledged that in an independent University of Manchester the Department of History would seek to remedy that defect.[2]

They soon had their chance. In 1904–05 a new university was created in Manchester. On 9 May 1905 the Board of the Faculty of Arts appointed committees for every Honours school, consisting in every case of the members of the faculty engaged in teaching and examining in the school. These committees were directed to revise the regulations and syllabuses of their respective Honours schools. Tout and Tait were given *carte blanche*.[3] They were offered an unrivalled opportunity to develop the school along their own by now clearly defined lines. Unlike Firth, Tout did not have to battle against a system stiffened by tradition to the point of inflexibility. In his campaign to secure a sound training in historical method for all undergraduates this was the most important factor in Tout's favour. A comparison of the process of change at Manchester with that at Oxford and Cambridge is instructive. It reveals clearly the way in which existing institutions and the consensus of opinion within them as to the function they are engaged in performing exert a powerful influence on the direction of change. When the University of Manchester was granted its charter in 1904 the idea that it had an active duty to encourage scientific and scholarly research was accepted and clearly understood. An institution which grew up with this belief did not have to undergo painful modifications in order to make practical provision for it.

Though it was unlikely, Tout made any opposition to his forthcoming proposals more problematical by stressing continually the educational value of research skills. 'The educational value of our study,' he said:

lies not so much in the accumulation of a mass of unrelated facts as in training in method, and evidence, and in seeing how history is made. It follows, then, that the study of history should be largely a study of processes and method, even for those to whom history is not mainly the preparation for a career, but chiefly a means of academic education. No historical education can, therefore, be regarded as complete unless it involves training in method. The best training in method is an attempt at research.[4]

While Tout aimed to promote 'a good scheme for teaching general historical knowledge to undergraduates' his definition of a general historical knowledge included instruction in the essential methods of historical research. By maintaining that teaching research principles was part of a general education, and would help develop the mind and faculties, he combined the two functions of the university – education and research – without stressing one unduly to the detriment of the other.

The meetings and discussions of 1905 brought few immediate changes to the syllabus. But two tentative suggestions were made. The first was based on the success achieved at Cambridge by dividing the Tripos, something which Tout called a 'sound and intelligible principle' that 'has surely come to stay'. A preliminary examination was proposed, and then put into practice informally, at the end of the student's second year, before serious work on the special subjects was begun. It was made formal and the results were published in 1909.

The second principle was that which Firth had established at Oxford – that any original work would be taken into account in the Final examination.[5] Tout was working gradually towards making a thesis compulsory for all students and a formal part of the Manchester history syllabus. But he heeded Ward's advice. Before committing the reputation of the school he tested the temperature of the academic water. At the request of Mary Bateson he delivered a provocative and forthright speech to the Newnham College History Society, copies of which were forwarded to leading historians all round the country.[6]

'The spirit of research is in the air,' said Tout. 'It has become a commonplace that it is the function of the historical professor, not only to teach, but also to write books.' This was an improvement on the conditions under which Stubbs and Seeley worked. But, he warned, 'all is not quite yet as it should be', for England lacked schools of history in the Continental sense. A school of history was not simply 'a good scheme for teaching general historical knowledge to undergraduates plus a respectable examination at the end of it'. Important as such preliminary knowledge undoubtedly was, on its own it tended towards 'the encouragement of mere smartness and readiness'. The 'true test' of academic success was 'not memory work but knowledge of method and criticism', and an examination that would test a student's understanding and intellectual dexterity. Tout was quite adamant. 'Most of our present systems,' he said:

> neglect the opportunity that lies at their doors, and content themselves with a perfunctory 'special period', which is either studied so early that the student is not ripe for it, or so imperfectly that he never realises the training that he can derive from it.

The special might work if the men were left to their own devices, but this rarely happened. It was common knowledge that many lecturers offered:

> the pupil a series of cut-and-dried lectures with all the obvious points systematically worked up, so all he has got to do is to read up his note-books and pour out on paper the treasures heaped up for him by others.

This form of teaching – which the Oxford examiners had chastised – by-passed the very purpose of the special subject. The student ought to be involved in active not passive work. The 'best way' to achieve this aim was:

> for the students to be formed into little groups not exceeding a dozen, and to put each group under the direction of a teacher who has already made the subject his own, and who is still engaged in working upon it.

All teaching should be based in a library, on the seminar method, and the student should be 'encouraged to write some sort of modest thesis . . . a practicable compromise between the German dissertation and the British examinations.' This system said Tout, would:

be eminently educative, so much so that it would train the minds of those who only use history as the means of education, as well as of those who would be led on by such a system to desire a more technical training after they had taken their degree . . .

. . . I cannot conceive how such a system would sacrifice the many to the few. It would be as good for the statesman, the lawyer, the clergyman, the journalist, the civil servant, and the man of business, as for the would-be historian.[7]

Replies were many and various. Some academics doubted the wisdom of Tout's words. E. A. Armstrong urged caution. He felt that the examination system had great value, and the special subject was no exception. 'It seems to me a good enough test of ability,' he said:

for after all for most professions, even for the future historian, it is a good practice to thoroughly accumulate a considerable bulk of knowledge and to be able to produce such parts of it as are required at a given moment in a limited space and time in good form, and that . . . more or less their own.[8]

Many silently believed Tout to be a Firth-like fanatic hell-bent on the destruction of the traditional university. Some believed that only the very best men could possibly benefit from the rigours of a thesis, and they were the men most likely to go on to a postgraduate course.[9]

But many agreed wholeheartedly with the idea. G. W. Prothero spoke for them when he said:

your plea for training in method without being too technical and in a style which would be equally good for all sorts and conditions of men, not for professional historians only is admirable.[10]

Others, while they agreed with that judgement, reflected on the difficulties facing Firth and Bury. R. L. Poole lamented sadly:

I agree with almost all your . . . suggestions; and it is only when I come to meditate on the possibility of fitting them into the Oxford system that I realise the immense power of accumulated tradition.[11]

Tout had freedom to express his ideas in a developing institutional context. Further, supervising theses did not involve the Manchester teachers in any fundamental change of habit, style or mode of work. Nor did it threaten their livelihood. Tout, Tait and later Unwin simply directed students to their own research interests. Tout was quite aware of his fortunate position. 'Freedom,' he said, 'is the *sine qua non* for success. 'What we want in the teaching of history,' he said:

> ... is the courage to make experiments combined with the courage to stand fast in what is good in the ancient ways. We must have above all things freedom to work out our salvation for ourselves.[12]

Nevertheless, Tout had taken advantage of the conditions in his favour and through a mixture of tact, patience and sheer hard work succeeded in putting his ideas into practice. After a short, informal, experimental period the thesis became in 1909 a vital and distinguishing feature of the school.

It was not always done well. Surviving examples show a great disparity in standards. The good ones, like that completed by Mark Hovell in 1909, show considerable command of historical technique and method, if not always a commensurate command of English. But the less able, like that written by Sarah Matthias a year earlier, are poor, lacking footnotes, bibliography and any discernable knowledge of authorities. Clearly Tout's help did not extend to doing the students' work for them. But Tout was pleased with the results. And on two distinct counts. For some students the thesis was clearly an excellent introduction to further historical work. For others it was a valuable means of encouraging 'independence' and 'self-help'. It is also interesting to note that in Tout's time no student ever took a First without securing an alpha grade on their thesis.[13] Equally, however, there were many others who produced what were adjudged First Class theses but who were awarded a Second or upper Second Class degree overall. Tout was keen to balance a thorough training in method with other more general skills. The employment statistics are interesting.

Bar those female students who married on graduation, all Tout's graduates found paid employment. Of the eighty who passed through the school between 1905 and 1914, six became teachers of history in universities or colleges. An impressive figure, but one that hardly outshines the record of the older schools in this respect. Whether it is a reflection on his teaching or not, Tout did not produce any statesmen in this period, nor – perhaps more to his general satisfaction – any journalists. Two took the cloth, two became members of the legal profession, another four became civil servants, two of them 'high-flyers'. Only one went into business. Most significant, however, was the school's imput into the teaching profession. Eighteen of the men (48·7%) and thirty-four of the women (80·62%) went back into schools to develop the study of history there. Manchester history graduates got jobs, and jobs which might be classed as 'professional'. But they were, generally speaking, of a lower status than those taken by their Oxford and Cambridge counterparts. Again more detailed work on the social backgrounds of Manchester graduates is required before we can be sure what contributed to this state of affairs. But preliminary study suggests strongly that Manchester students were drawn for the most part from the middle class. The reasons are conjectural but probably result from a combination of difficulties: poor local opportunities for secondary education, the high cost of private education, few scholarships to Owens College, and lack of appreciation of the nature and benefits of higher education. It seems that, as at Oxford, there was very little social mobility, either upwards or downwards, but that most students took up an occupation of the same social status as their parents. For most, a university education was a way of preserving or consolidating social position. These are matters which will become much clearer as work currently in progress is completed.[14]

Tout, however, was sufficiently impressed with his school and its graduates to claim in 1920 that:

> it is the boast of Manchester that the concluding year of its honours course forms a better bridge towards the advanced study of history than any other university of the kingdom.[15]

There were some who disagreed. Oxford and Cambridge boasted their share of academic historians, many of whom were developing the study in the new civic universities and colleges.[16] They were ambivalent about the thesis.[17] Some introduced it. Some did not. At London, which was beginning to develop a school to rival that of Manchester and the ancient universities, detailed technical training – agreed to be important – was left until the postgraduate stage. Pollard and his colleagues believed that the problems of co-ordinating the resources of the various far-flung colleges, of matching students with supervisors, and indeed of securing agreement among a large body of college teachers, made this the most practical solution. Pollard concentrated his energies into developing a first-rate graduate school.[18] 'The conclusion to be drawn,' said Richard Lodge, 'is not that this system is the best for all men, but that it is the best for Tout.'[19]

The importance of these elements of disagreement emanating from Oxford and Cambridge cannot lightly be discounted. They cast a number of qualifications on the less temperate statements made by recent historians of academic change in late nineteenth-century England. Professor Heyck, for instance, suggests that:

> By 1900 Oxford and Cambridge had become places where research and specialised study by a secular as well as a professional body of scholars and scientists dominated the terrain.[20]

This metamorphosis, he claims, was most evident in history, and due in great measure to the fact that college lecturers 'sought to erect career structures for themselves as university teachers', and cherished their new and prestigious duty of adding to knowledge.'[21]

Sheldon Rothblatt maintains that by the turn of the century the idea of a mental training was no longer the primary function of the university, and 'the outstanding features of Oxford and Cambridge that produced their claim to be the home of a liberal education' were 'the recreations and social life of the colleges; the balls, the games, the parties and picnics near the river, the performances of music and plays. . . .'[22] He suggests that in an attempt to push the university back into the forefront of national life, a desire not unconnected to a very general wish to create prestige for themselves, the dons had ensured that the curriculum became more directly vocational.[23]

Such claims, had they been made in 1900, would undoubtedly have raised a quizzical eyebrow from Firth and Bury. For them, Oxford and Cambridge were places where research took a secondary place. By 1900 it had hardly attained the status of an industry. Had it done so, then their campaign for the inclusion of research skills in the syllabus leading to a degree would hardly have been necessary. Dons had indeed sought for themselves careers as teachers, and this proved the source of greatest opposition to Firth and Bury's proposals. Research skills were not part of the qualifications required in a college teacher, and as a body college teachers defined their own function with that point very firmly in mind. They claimed that they were paid to guide students towards a fuller understanding of history and at the same time to ensure that they passed their examinations in such a way as to bring credit to themselves, their college and their parents. The tutors claimed credibility in their self-determined function by appealing to the concept, generally well understood, of a liberal education. This stressed the idea of the university as a place which sought to educate. They defined education as being directed to the supreme end of mental training. The chief pursuit of the university and the first aim of the history school within it was to develop the intellect in such a way as to adapt it to the more efficient pursuit of any calling, be it commerce, law, business, teaching or the church.[24]

Firth and Bury received a good deal of sympathy for their objectives. But the fate of their proposals revealed that in the general business of education there was still a clear distinction between teaching and research, particularly between teaching undergraduates general history and teaching them research techniques. It was a distinction which almost all college teachers – even those who taught and wrote – recognised. Perhaps the words of Sir Charles Oman convey most clearly the dominance of the traditional idea of teaching which persisted in the older universities:

The first problem that must be faced is that this University is a place of Education as well as a place of Research. It is sometimes difficult to correlate its two functions: it often seems difficult to determine how far they can or ought to be discharged by the same body of workers. But, whatever may be our views on this point, there remains the obvious fact that we are confronted by a large body of young men who have to be educated, and that the larger proportion of them are intended for careers for which no technical Schools-curriculum exists. For this let us be thankful; I shudder to think that there are fanatics who would be prepared to draw up the regulations for a special education for any line of life – journalism, the Stock Exchange, politics, Charity Organization, or the life of the country gentleman. But this madness is still far off – practically our problem is to deal with some 150 or 200 undergraduates destined for the most various occupations in after-life, who unite in thinking that the Modern History School suits them better than any other of the avenues to a degree which the University at present offers. Of this body a very small proportion are destined in the end to take up the burden of original research. I agree with Professor Firth – so doubtless does everyone here present – in regretting that the percentage is so small; but it can never be much larger – unless indeed some strange power should ever succeed in turning our old Modern History Course into a technical school for historians – technical in the sense that the education here in Medicine or Forestry is technical. I should myself . . . deplore any such transformation, holding as I do that the School is discharging a more generally useful function as it stands at present, than it would if it were equipped with a severely specialistic curriculum, intended only for those who were destined for the career of researchers in or teachers of history. Clearly a School reconstructed on such lines would cease to attract some four-fifths of those who at present enter for it. It would be a wholly different affair.[25]

In conclusion Oman pronounced that:

We must frankly recognise that the Modern History curriculum must be drawn up rather with an eye to the vast majority of men who seek in it a general liberal education, than to the small minority to whom a technical training . . . might conceivably be more profitable.[26]

While Tout was able to dissent from this view, Oman's words explain clearly why despite strong academic pressures the history syllabus underwent few sweeping changes at Oxford after 1870 or Cambridge after 1895. The traditional idea of a liberal education as the training of the mind – an idea formulated in the early nineteenth century – did not die. On the contrary it prevailed and flourished long beyond the nineteenth century. Far from being acquired through the pursuit of social graces and the attainment of a degree of cultivated levity, a liberal education was to be gained through a thorough and systematic course of study. The concept of mental training retained its power as the *raison d'être* of higher education because it was convenient for many academics that it did so. It offered them a powerful, well defined and widely accepted criterion by which to explain their own social function, and by which to maintain control of their own teaching profession. So it was that while the Oxbridge system undoubtedly broadened during the second half of the nineteenth century, in terms of the role and

function it defined for itself with respect to the education of undergraduates, little changed.

NOTES TO CHAPTER 8

1 John Rylands University Library of Manchester, Tout, 1/1242/58–59, Ward to
Tout, 7–8 August 1895. 1/367/28, Firth to Tout, 10 April 1892. 1/1242/32, Ward to Tout,
31 October 1892.
2 John Rylands University Library of Manchester, Tout, 1/.962/18–18, Powicke to
Tout, N.D. 1902. *Historical Essays by Members of the Owens College Manchester. Published in
Commemoration of the Jubilee (1851–1901)*, ed. T. F. Tout and James Tait (Manchester,
1902), p. xii.
3 University of Manchester, Archives, Minute Book of Proceedings of the Board
of Faculty of Arts, vol. 1, Min. 9 May 1905, Min. 6 June 1905 (p. 88).
4 Tout, 'An historical laboratory', in *Collected Papers*, p. 80.
5 U.M., B.F.A. Minutes, vol. 1, p. 114, p. 284; p. 288.
6 John Rylands University Library of Manchester, Tout, 1/71/8, Bateson to Tout,
6 October 1905.
7 Tout, *Schools of History* (p. 5) (p. 6) (p. 14) (p. 16).
8 John Rylands University Library of Manchester, Tout, 1/31/9, E. A. Armstrong
to Tout, 26 May 1906.
9 *Henry William C. Davis, 1874–1928: a Memoir by J. R. H. Weaver and a Selection of his
Historical Papers edited by J. R. H. Weaver and A. L. Poole* (London, 1933), p. 68.
10 John Rylands University Library of Manchester, Tout, 1/975/20, G. W. Prothero
to Tout, 25 May 1906.
11 John Rylands University Library of Manchester, Tout, 1/953/57 R. L. Poole to
Tout, 21 May 1906.
12 John Rylands University Library of Manchester, Tout, MS. notes on the
'Teaching of History' dated 11 February 1903 with note 9. 2. 1907 (p. 2).
13 University of Manchester, Department of History, Archive, Manchester University History School from 1882 (an Examiners' notebook). M. Woodcock (1911), H.
L. Beales (1912) and T. P. Spencer (1914) all took Seconds but scored First Class marks
on their thesis.
14 These figures are computed from record cards in the University of Manchester
Department of History departmental office. I am currently working in more detail on
social class, academic record and occupational status of Manchester graduates.
15 Tout, 'The Manchester School of History', in *Collected Papers*, vol. 1, pp. 85–9 (p.
88).
16 In 1914 for instance, twenty-seven Oxford graduates were teaching history in
the civics and in London.
17 Leeds, Liverpool, Bristol and Birmingham developed the thesis, Sheffield and
London did not.
18 For London see Pollard, 'The University of London' and Harte, *One Hundred and
Fifty Years*. For the problems see John Rylands University Library of Manchester, Tout,
1/672/109–110, S. Lee to Tout, 30 January, 7 February 1901.
19 Richard Lodge, 'Thomas Frederick Tout: a retrospect of twin academic
careers', *Cornhill Magazine*, No. 403, 1930, pp. 114–26 (p. 124).
20 Heyck, *The Transformation of Intellectual Life*, p. 172.
21 Heyck, p. 223.
22 Rothblatt, *Tradition and Change*, pp. 142–3 (p. 142).
23 Rothblatt, *Revolution of the Dons*, p. 250.
24 All Souls College, Oxford, 9.2.6.32(2), pp. 4–5.
25 Oman, *Inaugural Lecture on the Study of History*, pp. 18–19.
26 Oman, *Inaugural*, p. 21.

BIBLIOGRAPHY

1. MS. AND PRINTED EPHEMERA

A. OXFORD

(i) BODLEIAN LIBRARY

(a) *Oxford University archives*

NEP/subtus. Register of Convocation, 1846–54

wp Ɣ /24/1–7. Hebdomadal Registers, 1738–1866

wp Ɣ /27/1–4. Hebdomadal Registers, 1866–1908

wp Ɣ /28/1. Hebdomadal Council Reports, 1855–65

MH/M/1/1–3. Board of the Faculty of Arts (Modern History) Minute Books, 1883–1930

MH/RI/1–2. Board of the Faculty of Arts (Modern History) Reports, 1889–1921

UR/L38/3. Modern History Examiners' notebook, vol. I, 1900–37

(b) *Library collection*

  i MS. Top Oxon. c. 663. Papers of H. H. Vaughan as Regius Professor of Modern History

  MS. Eng. Lett. d. 435, d. 437. Letters of H. H. Vaughan

  MS. Eng. Lett. d. 440–441. Letters of H. H. Vaughan

  ii *Guard books*

  G. A. Oxon. b.26, b.30, b.138 (fol. 82), b.140 (fol. 55a, 67.b, 67.c, 67.d), b.141 (fol. 87a), c.65 (fol. 36, 37–43, 17a), c.70 (fol. 170), c.73 (fol. 331), c.79 (fol. 211, 416–17, 428.)

(ii) COLLEGE LIBRARIES

(a) *All Souls College*

G2.6.32(2). E. Armstrong and 22 others, *To C. H. Firth, M.A.*

G2.6.32(3). C. H. Firth, *I must begin by apologising.*

(b) *Balliol College*

  i MS. collection

  The A. L. Smith papers. Section I (a) 3–7, 8, 12, 13, (b) 3–4, (c) 2.

  ii *Pamphlet collection*

  Ernest Barker, *On the need for the re-distribution of the work prescribed for the School of Modern History* (1908)

A. L. Smith, *English Constitutional History from the beginning to 1307*

(c) *Exeter College*
c.iv.6. Schools' results
c.iv.8. College Lectures, 1855–77
J.I.1–21. C. W. Boase Papers
J.II.1–6. C. W. Boase Papers
College History Box 5, L.II 6. C. W. Boase Papers
College History Box 6. L.II 7. C. W. Boase Papers

(d) *Merton College*
P/2/17. Reports of College Committees

(e) *New College*
(i) *Archives*
9639–46. T. R. Press. Shelves 3, 4. Minute Book of Stated General Meetings, 1865–1940
9647–8. T. R. Press. Shelf 4. Minutes of Meetings of Warden and Tutors, 1865–68
(ii) *Library*
D.380 *The following are replies to a circular letter of enquiry* (Oxford, 1873)

(f) *Oriel College*
Letter Book 3, 201–300, No. 292. Hawkins to Whateley, 22 December 1849
N.3.24. *Hawkins Pamphlet Collection*
Hints on the formation of a plan for the safe and effectual revival of the professional system in Oxford (1839)
N.3.26. *The New Examination Statutes; with a catalogue of books* (Oxford, 1852)

B. CAMBRIDGE

(i) UNIVERSITY LIBRARY

(a) *Cambridge University Archives*
Guard Book C.U.R. 28.8 (Moral Sciences Tripos), 1848–1925
Guard Book C.U.R. 28.10 (Historical Tripos), 1868–1902
Guard Book C.U.R. 28.10.1, 1903–1926
Guard Book C.U.R. 39.14 (Professor of Modern History), 1628–1954
min. vi. 6. Minutes of Syndicates, 1849–1900
min. vi. 9. University Studies Syndicates, 1853–54
min. v. 10. Board of Moral Science Studies (Minutes)
UP 13 (1837–53) UP 17 (1847–49), fols. 801–2, 821–5, 828–9, 839–40, 917, 959, 1051
UP 21 (1852–55), fols. 879. 884
UP 28 (1858–60), fols. 1158, 1170

UP 40 (1867), fol. 80, fol. 344
UP 41 (1867–83) fol. 134
UP 60, fols. 49–50 357–62, 374–85

(b) *Library Collection*
Add 7349/1/1–45. Letters of Sir J. Stephen to J. F. Stephen.
Add. 7888. Biographical Collections of Sir J. Stephen
Add. 8119/1. Acton Correspondence
Add. 6443 (e). Acton Correspondence

(c) *Cambridge Papers*
DC 5650 (Moral Sciences). W. G. Clark. 22 February 1859.

(ii) SEELEY HISTORICAL LIBRARY

Minutes of the Special Board for History and Archaeology, vol. 1,
        1876–93; vol. II, 1893–1927
Historical Tripos. Examiners' Book, November 1888 – June 1910

(iii) COLLEGES

(a) *Emmanuel College*
Col. 9. 39. A–E. H. M. Gwatkin Papers
Tut 4 1–3. Minutes of the Educational Board

(b) *King's College*
Q. 32 Ref 33. J. P. Whitney. *Sir George Walter Prothero as an Historian: an address
        given to a special meeting of the Royal Historical Society Nov. 23 1922*
Minutes of King's College Educational Council, 1861–82, (in 2 vols.)
Minutes of King's College Council, 1882–1901 (4 vols.)

(c) *St John's College*
C. cl. 1. Minutes of St John's College Education Board, 1860–82
C. cl. 2–3. Minutes of St John's College Education Committee, 1882–99
C. 5 4. St John's College Conclusion Book, 1847–73
D. 100. 77. Inter-collegiate Examination in History
D. 104. 109–17. Inter-collegiate Lecture Scheme.
P. 6.1. St John's College Examination Papers

(d) *Trinity College*
Add. MS. A. 212. 179–182, 184–197. Letters of Sir James Stephen to W.
        Whewell, April 1849 – April 1859
303. 6.1. Trinity College Examination Papers

C. MANCHESTER

(i) JOHN RYLANDS UNIVERSITY LIBRARY OF MANCHESTER
Papers of T. F. Tout. Edited with an introduction by Peter Slee

UA/2/37. Draft schemes of Examinations and Class attendance in divers Honours Schools

(ii) FACULTY OF ARTS
Victoria University of Manchester. Minute Book of the Proceedings of the Board of the Faculty of Arts, vol. 1, 1903–

(iii) DEPARTMENT OF HISTORY
Manchester University History School from 1882 (an examiners' notebook)

D. LONDON

(a) Royal Historical Society. University College
     Papers of G. W. Prothero
(b) Institute of Historical Research
     Papers of J. R. Seeley

2. ROYAL COMMISSION AND SELECT COMMITTEE REPORTS, AND RETURNS TO THE HOUSE OF COMMONS

Report of the Commissioners appointed to inquire into the State, Discipline, Studies and Revenues of the University and Colleges of Oxford, 1852 (1482) XXII, 1.

Report of the Commissioners appointed to inquire into the State, Discipline, Studies and Revenues of the University and Colleges of Cambridge, 1852–53, XLIV, 1

Special Report from the Select Committee on the Oxford and Cambridge Universities Education Bill, 1867, XIII, 183

Return from the Universities of Oxford and Cambridge . . . for each year from 1870 to 1875 inclusive, 1876, LIX, 327

Return to an Address of the Honourable the House of Commons dated May 25th 1876, 1876, LIX, 35.

Evidence taken by Commissioners . . . and circulars addressed by Commissioners to University and Colleges with answers, 1881, LV. 1

Return from the Universities of Oxford and Cambridge, 1886, LI, 519

Report of the Royal Commission Appointed to Inquire into the Depression of Trade and Industry, 1886, XXI–XII

3. UNPUBLISHED THESES, ETC.

Slee, P. R. H., History as a Discipline at the Universities of Oxford and Cambridge, 1848–1914. (Cambridge Ph.D.,1983).

4. PUBLISHED WORKS

(a) BEFORE 1914

Abbott, E., and Campbell, L., The Life and Letters of Benjamin Jowett, M.A. (in two volumes) (London, 1897)

Acton, J. E. E. D., 'German schools of history', E.H.R., 1, 1885, 7–42

— Lectures on Modern History, edited with an introduction by J. N. Figgis and R. V. Laurence (London, 1906)

Adamson, J. W., 'Education', in The Cambridge History of English Literature, edited by A. W. Ward and A. R. Waller, XIV, pp. 381–433

Appleton, C. E. C. B., ed., Essays on the Endowment of Research (London, 1876)

Archbold, W. A. J., ed., Essays on the Teaching of History (Cambridge, 1901)

Arnold, T., Inaugural Lecture on the Study of Modern History, December 2nd 1841 (Oxford, 1841)

Ashley, W. J., 'Modern history at Oxford', in European Schools of History and Politics, ed. A. D. White (Johns Hopkins University Studies in Historical and Political Science) 5th series, 12, 1887 (Baltimore, 1887), pp. 45–55

Bede, C., pseud., The Adventures of Mr. Verdant Green, an Oxford Undergraduate (1853)

Bernard, M., A Letter to the Vice Chancellor on the Provision for the Teaching of Law at Oxford (Oxford, 1864)

Blakesley, J. W., Where does the Evil Lie? Observations Addressed to the Resident Members of the Senate, on the Prevalence of Private Tuition in the University of Cambridge (London, 1845)

Brown, C. E., Letter to a Friend upon the Proposed Additions to the Academical System of Education October 15th 1848 (Cambridge, 1848)

Browning, O., 'The Historical Tripos', Cambridge Review, VI, 140, 4 February 1885, 178–80

— The Proposed New Historical Tripos (London, 1896)

— Memories of Sixty Years, at Eton, Cambridge and Elsewhere (London, 1910)

Burrows, M., Pass and Class: an Oxford Guide Book through the Courses of Literae Humaniores, Mathematics, Natural Science and Law and Modern History (Oxford, 1860)

— Is Educational Reform required in Oxford, and What? (Oxford, 1859)

— Inaugural Lecture 30 October 1802 (Oxford, 1862)

— Autobiography of Montagu Burrows, edited by S. M. Burrows (London, 1908)

Bury, J. B., An Inaugural Lecture: Delivered in the Divinity School, Cambridge, on 26 January, 1903 (Cambridge, 1903)

Carlyle, T., 'On history', Fraser's Magazine, 2, No. 10, 1830, 413–18

— 'Memoirs of the life of Walter Scott', London and Westminster Review, 30, 1838, 293–340

Congreve, R., Historical Lectures (London, 1900)

Copleston, E., A Reply to the Calumnies of the Edinburgh Review, containing an Account of studies pursued in that University, 2nd edition (London, 1810)

Copleston, W. J., Memoir of Edward Copleston, D.D., Bishop of Llandaff, with Selections from his Diary and Correspondence (London, 1851)

Courtney, W. L., 'Oxford tutors and their professional critic', Fortnightly Review, 53, 1890, 294–6

Creighton, L., ed., Life and Letters of Mandell Creighton [in two volumes] (London, 1904).

Creighton, M., The Teaching of Ecclesiastical History, Inaugural Lecture at the University of Cambridge (Cambridge, 1885)

Curzon, G. N., Principles and Methods of University Reform: being a Letter addressed to the University of Oxford (Oxford, 1909)

Daubeny, C., Brief Remarks on the Correlation of the Natural Sciences (Oxford, 1848)

Dodgson, C. L., The New Examination Statute (Oxford, 1864)

Douglas, S., The Life and Selections from the Correspondence of William Whewell, D.D., late Master of Trinity College, Cambridge (London, 1881)

Drosier, W. H., Remarks on the New Regulations Recommended by the Syndicate of October 27th, 1859 for the Moral and Natural Sciences Examinations (Cambridge, 1860)

Dublin Review, 'The Irish and English universities', 1 May 1836, 68–100

Edinburgh Review, 'Traité mechanique céleste par P. S. La Place', XI, No. XXII, 1808, 249–84

— 'The Oxford Edition of Strabo', XIV, No. XXVIII, 1809, 429–41

— "Essays on a professional education by R. L. Edgeworth', XV, No. XXIX, 1809, 40–53

Elton, E., Frederick York Powell, a Life and Selections from his Letters and Occasional Writings [in two volumes] (Oxford, 1906)

Farrar, F. W., ed., Essays on a Liberal Education (London, 1867)

Firth, C. H., Honours in History (Oxford, 1903)

— A Plea for the Historical Teaching of History: an Inaugural Lecture Delivered on 9 November 1904 (Oxford, 1904)

— The Faculties and their Powers: a Contribution to the History of University

Organisation (Oxford, 1909)

— 'The study of modern history in Great Britain', P.B.A., VI, 1913, 139–150

Fisher, H. A. L., ed., *The Collected Papers of F. M. Maitland* [in three volumes] (Cambridge, 1911)

Foster, J., *Alumni Oxoniensis*, volumes 1–5 (London, 1888)

Fredericq, P., 'The study of history in England and Scotland'

Johns Hopkins Studies in Historical and Political Science, 5th series, 10 (Baltimore, 1887)

Freeman, E. A., *Thoughts on the Study of History, with Reference to the proposed Changes in the Public Examinations* (Oxford, 1849)

— 'Historical study at Oxford', Bentley's Quarterly 1, 1859, 282–300

— 'Oxford after Forty Years', Contemporary Review, 51, 1887, 609–23, 814–830

Freeman, E. A., and Boase, C. W., *Correspondence between the Protestant Alliance and the Examiners in Law and Modern History* (Oxford, 1858)

Froude, J. A., 'Suggestions on the best means of Teaching English History', in *Oxford Essays* (London, 1855), pp. 47–80

Gardiner, S. R., and others, 'Oxford professors and Oxford tutors', Contemporary Review, LVII, 1890, 184–6

Gooch, G. P., *History and Historians in the Nineteenth Century* (London, 1913)

Green, J. R., 'Professor Stubbs's Inaugural Lecture', Saturday Review, 2 March 1867, 278–80

Gwatkin, H. M., 'The Historical Tripos', Cambridge Review, VI, 141, 15 February 1885, 199–200

— *The Meaning of Ecclesiastical History: an Inaugural Lecture* (Cambridge, 1891)

Haddan, T. H., *Remarks on Legal Education, with Reference to the suggested Introduction of Legal Studies into the University of Oxford* (London, 1858)

Hammond, B. E., 'Law and history', Cambridge Review, V, No. 110, 10 December 1883, 123–4

— 'The Historical Tripos', in *The Student's Guide to the University of Cambridge* (third edition) (Cambridge, 1874), pp. 421–38.

Hooper, J. J., *The Establishment of a School of Jurisprudence in the University of Oxford* (Oxford, 1854)

Hort, A. F., *Life and Letters of F. J. A. Hort* [in two volumes] (London, 1896)

Hutton, W. H., ed., *Letters of William Stubbs: Bishop of Oxford, 1825–1901* (London, 1904)

Huxley, T. H., *Collected Essays*, Volume III (London, 1893)

Johnson, A. H., *Faculty of Arts, Honour School of Modern History Historical Account* (Oxford, 1900)

[Jowett, B., and Stanley, A. P.,] *Suggestions for an Improvement of the Examination Statute* (Oxford, 1848)

Kingsley, C., *The Roman and the Teuton* (London, 1864)

Lily, W. S., 'The new spirit in history', Nineteenth Century, XXI, 1895, 619–31

Lodge, R., The Study of History in a Scottish University: an Inaugural Lecture, delivered on 22 October 1894 (Glasgow, 1894)

Luard, H. R., Suggestions on . . . the Establishment of an Historical Tripos (Cambridge, 1866)

Marsh, W., Remarks on the University System of Education (Cambridge, 1848)

Mayor, J. B., 'The Moral Sciences Tripos', in The Student's Guide to the University of Cambridge (Cambridge, 1863), pp. 140–52

— Remarks on Proposals to grant the Degree of B.A. to persons who have obtained Honours in the Moral Sciences Tripos (Cambridge, 1860)

Neate, C., Remarks on the Legal and other Studies of the University (Oxford, 1856)

Oman, C. W. C., Inaugural Lecture on the Study of History, 7 February 1906 (Oxford, 1906)

Palmer, R., Suggestions with regard to certain proposed Alterations in Oxford (Oxford, 1854)

Powell, F. Y., 'The Ecole des Chartes and English records', T.R.H.S. XI, 1897, 31–40

Price, L. L., The Present Position of Economic Study at the University of Oxford (Oxford, 1902)

Prothero, G. W., 'The Historical Tripos', Cambridge Review, VI, 139, 28 January 1895, 163–6

— 'The Historical Tripos: a reply', C.R., VI, 142, 11 February 1885, 200–1

— Why should we Learn History? An Inaugural Lecture delivered at Edinburgh, 18 October, 1894 (Edinburgh, 1894)

— Historical Societies in Great Britain, American Historical Association report, 1909 (Washington, D.C., 1909), pp. 229–42.

Pryme, G., A Syllabus of a Course of Lectures on the Principles of Political Economy (London, 1816)

Rogers, J. E. T., Education in Oxford: its Methods, its Aids and its Rewards (London, 1861)

— 'Reforms in the University of Oxford', British Quarterly Review, 70, 1879, 62–91

— 'Oxford professors and Oxford tutors', Contemporary Review, LVI, 1889, 926–36

— 'The four Oxford History Lecturers', Contemporary Review, LVII, 1890, 454–6

Roundell, C. S., Letter to the Vice Chancellor (Oxford, 1864)

Russell, G. W. D., ed., Letters of Matthew Arnold, 1848–88 (London, 1901)

Sedgwick, A., A Discourse on the Studies of the University (Cambridge, 1833)

Seeley, J. R., Classical Studies as an Introduction to the Moral Sciences: Inaugural Lecture, October, 1863 (London, 1864)

— Lectures and Essays (London, 1870)

— 'History and politics', *Macmillan's magazine*, 40, 1879, 289–99, 369–78, 499–508; 41, 1879, 28–52

— 'The Historical Tripos', *Cambridge Review*, VI, 141, 11 February 1885, 194–5

Shaw, W. A., *Selected Papers and Essays of R. C. Christie* (London, 1902)

Smith, A. L., 'The new History School', *Oxford Magazine*, 4, 10 February 1886, 36–7

Smith, J. J., *Reply to Mr Harper's Remarks* (Cambridge, 1848)

Stebbing, W., ed., *C. H. Pearson, Fellow of Oriel and Education minister in Victoria* (London, 1900)

Stephen, C. E., *The Right Hon. Sir James Stephen: Letters with Biographical Notes* (Gloucester, 1906)

Stephen, J., *Lectures on the History of France* [in two volumes] (London, 1851)

Stephen, L., *Life of Henry Fawcett* (London, 1885)

— *The Life of J. F. Stephen* (London, 1895)

Stubbs, W., *Select Charters* (Oxford, 1870)

— *Constitutional History of England* [in three volumes] (Oxford, 1874–78)

— *Seventeen Lectures on the Study of Medieval and Modern History*, third edition (Oxford, 1900)

Teacher, A., pseud., 'The new History School', *Oxford Magazine*, 4 January 1886, p. 12.

Theamon, pseud., 'The Historical Tripos, from an examiner's point of view', *Cambridge Review*, VI, 139, 28 January 1885, 162–3

Todhunter, I., *The Conflict of Studies and other Essays* (London, 1873)

Tout, T. F., *Schools of History* (Manchester, 1906)

Tout, T. F., and Tait, J., ed., *Historical Essays by Members of the Owens College, Manchester* (London, 1902)

Tweed, J. P., *Our Law Professorships and the Claims of the School of Law and Modern History* (Oxford, 1863)

Twiss, T., *A Letter to the Vice-Chancellor on the Law Studies of the University* (London, 1856)

Vaughan, H. H., *Two General Lectures on Modern History delivered on Inauguration, October, 1849* (Oxford, 1849)

Ward, A. W., 'The study of history at Cambridge', *Saturday Review*, 6 July 1872

— *Suggestions towards the Establishment of a History Tripos* (Cambridge, 1872)

— 'Presidential address', *T.R.H.S.*, XIV, 1900, 1–18

Whewell, W., *Of a Liberal Education in General and with Particular Reference to the Leading Studies of the University of Cambridge* (London, 1845)

— *Of a Liberal Education in General and with Especial Reference to the University of Cambridge*, Volume II (London, 1850)

White, G. C., *A Versatile Professor: Reminiscences of the Rev. Edward Nares, D.D.* (London, 1903)

(b) AFTER 1914

Adamson, J. W., 'Education', in *The Cambridge History of English Literature*, ed. A. W. Ward and A. R. Waller (Cambridge, 1914), vol. XIV, pp. 381–433

Anderson, O., 'The political uses of history in mid-nineteenth century England', *Past and Present*, 36, 1967, 87–105

Anstruther, I., *Oscar Browning: a biography* (London, 1983)

Baynes, N. H., *A Bibliography of the Works of J. B. Bury, with a Memoir* (Cambridge, 1929)

Benson, A. C., *Memories and Friends* (London, 1924)

Berdahl, R. O., *British Universities and the State* (London, 1959)

Bill, E. G. W., *University Reform in Nineteenth-century Oxford: a Study of Henry Halford Vaughan, 1811–1885* (Oxford, 1973)

Blaas, P. B. M., *Continuity and Anachronism: Parliamentary and Constitutional Development in Whig Historiography and the Anti-Whig Reaction between 1890 and 1930* (The Hague, 1978)

Brooks, R. A. E., 'The development of the historical mind', in *The Reinterpretation of Victorian Literature*, ed. J. E. Baker (Princeton, 1950), pp. 130–53

Buckley, J. H., *The Triumph of Time: a Study of the Victorian Concepts of Time, History, Progress and Decadence* (Cambridge, Mass., 1967)

Burrow, J. W., *A Liberal Descent: Victorian Historians and the English Past* (Cambridge, 1981)

Butler, K. T. B., 'A petty Professor of Modern History: William Smyth, 1765–1849', *Cambridge Historical Journal*, IX, 2, 1948, 217–38

Cavenagh, F. A., ed., *Herbert Spencer on Education* (Cambridge, 1932)

Chadwick, W. O., 'Charles Kingsley at Cambridge', *Historical Journal*, XVIII, 1975, 303–25

Clarke, M. L., *Classical Education in Britain, 1500–1900* (Cambridge, 1959)

Collini, S., Winch, D., and Burrow, J., *That Noble Science of Politics: a Study in Nineteenth-century Intellectual History* (Cambridge, 1983)

Cordeaux, E. H., and Merry, D. H., *Bibliography of Printed Works Relating to the University of Oxford* (Oxford, 1968)

Cunningham, A., *William Cunningham, Teacher and Priest* (London, 1950)

Dale, P. A., *The Victorian Critic and the Idea of History* (Cambridge, Mass., 1977)

Engel, A. J., *From Clergyman to Don: the Rise of the Academic Profession in Ninteenth Century Oxford* (Oxford, 1983)

Fifoot, C. H. S., ed., *The Letters of F. W. Maitland* (Cambridge, 1965)

Firth, C. H., 'Modern history in Oxford, 1724–1841', E.H.R., XXXII, 1917, 1–21

— *Modern History in Oxford, 1841–1918* (Oxford, 1920)

Fisher, H. A. L., *The Place of the University in National Life* (Barnett House Papers, No. 4) (London, 1919)

— *An Unfinished Autobiography* (London, 1940)

Garland, M. M., *Cambridge before Darwin: the Ideal of a Liberal Education, 1800–1860* (Cambridge, 1980)

Gooch, G. P., 'The Cambridge Chair of modern history', in *Studies in Modern History by G. P. Gooch* (London, 1931), pp. 896–919

— *Under Six Reigns* (London, 1958)

Heitland, W. E., *After many years* (Cambridge, 1926)

Heyck, T. W., *The Transformation of Intellectual Life in Victorian England* (London, 1982)

Higham J., with Krieger, L., and Gilbert, F., *History: the Development of Historical Studies in the United States* (Princeton, 1965)

Humphreys, R. A., *The Royal Historical Society, 1868–1968* (London, 1969)

Jenkins, H., and Caradog Jones, D., 'The social class of Cambridge University alumni of the eighteenth and nineteenth centuries', *British Journal of Sociology*, 1, 1950, 93–116

Jenkyns, R., *The Victorians and Ancient Greece* (Oxford, 1980)

Johnson, A. H., 'The Modern History Association', *Oxford Magazine*, 7, November 1919, 63–4

Kitson Clark, G., 'A hundred years of the teaching of history at Cambridge, 1873–1973', *Historical Journal*, 16, 1973, 535–53

Lawson, F. H., *The Oxford Law School, 1850–1965* (Oxford, 1968)

Lodge, M. B., *Sir Richard Lodge: a Biography* (Edinburgh, 1946)

Lodge, R., 'Thomas Frederick Tout: a Retrospect of twin Academic Careers', *Cornhill Magazine*, LXVIII, 1930, 114–26

McClachlan, J. O., 'The origins and early development of the Cambridge Historical Tripos', *Cambridge Historical Journal*, 9, 1947–49, 78–105.

McPherson, R. G., *Theory of Higher Education in Nineteenth Century England* (Athens, N.Y., 1959)

Marriott, J. A. R., *Memories of Four Score Years* (London, 1946)

Marwick, A., *The Nature of History* (London, 1970)

Muir, R., *An Autobiography and some Essays*, edited by S. Hodgson (London, 1943)

Musgrove, F. 'Middle Class Education and Employment in the Nineteenth Century', *Economic History Review*, XII, 1959–60, 99–111

Myers, J. L., *The Provision for Historical Studies at Oxford* (Oxford, 1915)

Ogilvie, R. M., *Latin and Greek: a History of the Influence of the Classics on English Life from 1600 to 1918* (London, 1904)

Oman, C. W. C., *On the Writing of History* (London, 1939)

— *Memories of Victorian Oxford* (London, 1941)

Perkin, H., 'Middle class education and employment in the nineteenth century: a critical note', *Economic History Review*, XIV, 1961–62, 122–30

Pollard, A. F., 'The University of London and the study of history', in *Factors in*

Modern History, third edition (London, 1932)

Powicke, F. M., *Modern Historians and the Study of History* (London, 1955)

Reitlinger, G. R., *The Economics of Taste: the Rise and Fall of Picture Prices, 1760–1960* (London, 1961)

Rothblatt, S., *The Revolution of the Dons: Cambridge and Society in Victorian England* (London, 1968)

— *Tradition and Change in English Liberal Education: an Essay in History and Culture* (London, 1976)

Shils, E., *Tradition* (London, 1981)

Slee, P. R. H., 'A licence to slaughter: John Haviland and the reform of Cambridge medical education, 1817–1857', *Cambridge Medicine*, 2, 1980, 46–7

— 'The H. M. Gwatkin papers', *Proceedings of the Cambridge Bibliographical Society*, VIII, 1982, 279–84

— 'Concern for Skills', *Universities quarterly*, 40, No. 2, 1986, 163–70

Smith, M. F., *Arthur Lionel Smith, Master of Balliol, 1916–1924* (London, 1928)

Southern, R. W. 'The shape and substance of academic history', in *The Varieties of History from Voltaire to the Present*, ed. Fritz Stern (London, 1970), 403–23

Strong, R., *When did you last see your Father? The Victorian Painter and British History* (London, 1978)

Sutherland, G., 'The study of the history of education', *History*, LIV, 1969. 49–59

Sutherland, L. S., *The University of Oxford in the Eighteenth Century: a Reconsideration* (Oxford, 1973)

Tout, T. F., *The Collected Papers of T. F. Tout; with a memoir and bibliography* (Manchester, 1932)

Trevelyan, G. M., *An Autobiography and other Essays* (London, 1949)

Ward, W. R., *Victorian Oxford* (London, 1965)

Weaver, J. R. H., and Poole, A. L., ed., *Henry William C. Davis, 1874–1928: a Memoir* (London, 1933)

Winstanley, D. A., *Early Victorian Cambridge* (Cambridge, 1948)

— *Later Victorian Cambridge* (Cambridge, 1947)

Woodward, E. L., 'The rise of the professorial historian in England', in *Studies in International History, Essays presented to W. N. Medlicott*, ed. K. Bourne and D. C. Watt (London, 1967), pp. 16–34

Wormell, D., *Sir John Seeley and the Uses of History* (Cambridge, 1980)

Wortham, H. E., *Oscar Browning* (London, 1927)

INDEX